S0-BHR-797

REGIS COLLEGE
TORONTO
LIBRARY
WITHDRAWN

The Lopsided World

Books by Barbara Ward

THE WEST AT BAY

POLICY FOR THE WEST

FAITH AND FREEDOM

THE INTERPLAY OF EAST AND WEST

FIVE IDEAS THAT CHANGE THE WORLD

INDIA AND THE WEST

THE RICH NATIONS AND THE POOR NATIONS

NATIONALISM AND IDEOLOGY

THE LOPSIDED WORLD

BARBARA WARD

THE LOPSIDED WORLD

REGIS COLLEGE TORONTO LIBRARY WITHDRAWN

HC
59
.7
J26

The Christian A. Herter Lecture Series
Johns Hopkins University, School of Advanced International Studies
(Washington, D.C.)

W · W · NORTON & COMPANY · INC · *New York*

15083

SBN 393 05360 1   Cloth Edition
SBN 393 09805 2   Paper Edition

Copyright © 1968 by W. W. Norton & Company, Inc. All rights
reserved. Published simultaneously in Canada by George J. McLeod
Limited, Toronto. *Library of Congress catalog card no. 68-19328.*
Printed in the United States of America.

3 4 5 6 7 8 9 0

FOR
R. W. J.

Contents

Preface

IN 1964 the faculty of the Johns Hopkins School of Advanced International Studies established the Christian A. Herter Lecture Series in order to do honor to the distinguished American who had founded the School some twenty years earlier. It was the hope of the faculty that our lecture platform here in Washington might be used by highly qualified individuals to present different points of view about international relations and to examine in depth some of the basic issues that confront the United States in a rapidly changing world.

Some time later when I placed before Mr. Herter a list of three outstanding persons who might be invited to deliver the first lectures, there was not a moment's hesitation. Quickly and enthusiastically he selected the name of Barbara Ward.

Miss Ward graciously accepted our invitation. She chose as her topic "The Post-War Colonial World Economy," and in the spring of 1965 she inaugurated the Christian A. Herter Lecture Series by delivering three informal public lectures on The Economics of Plenty, The

Economics of Privation, and The Challenge of Economic Co-Existence.

From those three lectures Miss Ward has developed this penetrating and challenging little book, which she has chosen to call *The Lopsided World*. The fundamental thesis remains the same, but the lectures have been reorganized and brought up to date, and a good deal of new material has been added.

In these pages the author, in her warm and sprightly style, deals with one of the most important and most difficult problems that face mankind today — the development of the new nations. At the outset she reminds us that the affluent world, concentrated largely around the North Atlantic, each year adds to its existing wealth all and more of the entire income available to the other continents. Despite all our efforts since World War II, the alarming chasm between the rich nations and the poor nations grows ever wider and deeper.

Like the chef who knows precisely what ingredients to use, Miss Ward draws freely upon history to give perspective to her work. She explains the processes by which the wealthy nations have developed their economies over the years and then, skillfully drawing her lessons from the past, points out those things that need to be done to enable the poor states to join the charmed circle. Admittedly she is an activist; she sees a great and acute problem and she wants the leaders of the Western world to come to grips with it.

Even so, her analysis is an objective one. She explores, with keen insight, the mistakes that have been made, the reasons development programs have faltered, the progress that has been charted in the direction of modernization, and the prospects for the future. In her explorations she never loses sight of her main theme — what we need to do to accelerate the process of modernization and to apply to the poorer nations those methods and strategies that have proven themselves with respect to the development of the affluent countries.

It is not my purpose here to comment on the author's analysis of the problem or her prescriptions for the future. I cannot resist the temptation, however, to make one point about our own foreign-aid program that is prompted by her presentation. I can recall very well that when the Marshall Plan was launched in 1948, the United States contributed nearly $4 billion annually toward the reconstruction of a war-torn Europe. Very little of this was in the form of loans; most of it went as outright grants to the recipient countries. This represented about 1.5 per cent of our gross national product, which in 1948 was only $258 billion. The result was the almost miraculous recovery of Europe and new strength and hope for the Western world.

In the two decades since 1948 our gross national product has more than doubled in real terms. Despite this enormous growth and despite the great needs of the new countries, our foreign-aid program has been sharply curtailed. It still amounts to about the same $4 billion but the dollar is worth only two-thirds as much as it was twenty years ago. Today our foreign aid is less than 0.5 per cent of our gross national product of $800 billion. As George Woods, former president of the World Bank, pointed out early in 1968, the contributions of the wealthy countries for development purposes are large enough to irritate their legislative bodies but much too small to accomplish real economic progress.

Actually, our record is even less inspiring than appears on the surface. Virtually all of our assistance is now what is euphemistically called tied-aid — that is, it is devoted to the purchase of American products. Equally important is the often forgotten fact that much of it is now extended in the form of loans that eventually must be paid back by the recipient nations. Foreign aid has long since ceased to be a give-away program.

I am not suggesting that we once again devote 1.5 per cent (some $12 billion) of our gross national product to foreign-assistance programs. That would be completely unrealistic today in view of the other urgent demands on our federal budget. But it is quite apparent to me — as it must be to many other people — that what is needed is a dramatic proposal for a massive foreign-aid program that would fire the imagination, encourage the coopera-tion, and challenge the productive capacities of the countries involved as the Marshall Plan once did.

It is my hope that Barbara Ward's excellent book will do much to help the leaders of the rich nations and the poor nations alike to realize the nature of the tremendous challenge that faces us all in the lopsided world in which we live. From my close association with Christian Herter, I am sure that if he were alive today he would subscribe wholeheartedly to the sentiments expressed in these pages.

FRANCIS O. WILCOX, *Dean*
The Johns Hopkins School of
Advanced International Studies

Washington, D.C.
March 11, 1968

Chapter One

Fact and Context

I N THIS last third of the twentieth century the human species confronts a number of unprecedented facts. A small number of states, equaling some 20 per cent of the world's population, controls 80 per cent of the world's wealth. Their citizens have an individual (or per capita) income of above 600 dollars.* They are, in the main, white and post-Christian—but Japan is included. They are, in the main, market economies—although the Soviet Union is their most populous member. They live, in the main, round the North Atlantic ocean—although the offshoots of European colonization in Australasia and

* Details of national incomes can be studied in Appendix A.

(11)

South Africa belong to the charmed circle. Their combined annual national income of goods and services approaches $2,000,000 million of which their wealthiest member, the United States, accounts for about 40 per cent—or $800,000 million. And this wealth is dynamic. Each year it grows by about 3 per cent and adds not less than $60,000 million to existing incomes.

The gap between this wealthy group of states and the rest of mankind can perhaps be most vividly illustrated by comparing their $60,000 million annual increase with the *total* income of other areas. The combined national incomes of all the states in Latin America is not much above $60,000 million. The national income of India (with 500 million people) is only two thirds of that sum. The national income of Africa is lower still. In other words, the affluent world, largely concentrated round the North Atlantic, adds each year to its existing wealth all and more of the entire income available to other continents.

The reason for this difference is not that the developing nations—the two thirds of mankind who live outside the affluent group—do not grow at all. They do. The average increase in their national incomes, at 4.8 per cent a year, is higher than that of the North Atlantic world in the nineteenth century. But for every advance they make, the fully developed nations make a hundred more. The gap increases because they move at the speed of a bicycle, their wealthy neighbours at the speed of a moon rocket.

When, after the Second World War, the wealthy

peoples first became aware of this gap, they began to do something about it. A first modest step—President Truman's proposals for technical assistance, the so-called "Point Four" programs of 1949—had grown by the early nineteen-sixties to a transfer of genuine aid from rich to poor nations of some $6,000 million a year. The Atlantic Powers joined with the rest of the world in the United Nations to sponsor a Decade of Development. President Kennedy, young spokesman of a new generation, declared that aid should be given not simply from self interest but because it was morally right. It began to look as though the affluent powers were ready to add an extra dimension to their sense of responsibility and obligation. Having accepted the principle of "the general welfare" at home, they were ready to apply it to the whole family of man.

But today as the Decade draws to a close, it is not so certain. Since 1960, the Atlantic Powers have added at least $350,000 million to their combined national incomes. But their allocations for aid have not grown at all. As a result, economic assistance as a proportion of national income has fallen below 0.6 per cent of national incomes which still rise each year by at least 3 per cent. In some cases, notably that of America, the wealthiest state, the figure for aid is falling absolutely as well. In 1963, the U.S. allocation was $3,800 million. For 1967, it may be as little as $2,200 million. Small, brave countries like Canada or Holland may announce their intention to increase assistance and accept 1 per cent of national income as their norm. But they hardly offset the falling off of the big providers. Without a sharp and decided shift in emphasis and direction, it looks as though the policy of the richest powers in the seventies will be to grow wealthier themselves and do less for the poorer nations.*

There is no secret about the reasons for this change of direction. In general terms, the notion of a sustained effort of economic and social assistance on the behalf of other peoples way beyond the nation's boundaries is too new to be accepted as a matter of course. People are predisposed to believe that such an effort must be exceptionally successful and promise exceptional and speedy results for the "experiment" to be worth continuing. But given the bias in most reporting of world events, it is the failures that hit the headlines while the slower, deeper movements of change and modernization are less vividly reported. So the critics can point to any number of errors and breakdowns and argue from them the need to end the whole business of economic assistance.

This mood of impatience and rejection is reinforced by another set of preconceived ideas. The affluent peoples have, on the whole, very little knowledge of the conditions under which their own societies become technologically sophisticated, highly educated, and hence highly productive. Many of the decisive changes happened over a century ago. The present generation in the North Atlantic states hardly knows how long

* Details of the aid programmes of the countries associated with the Organization for Economic Cooperation and Development (OECD) are to be found in Appendix B.

such changes took or how they happened or what impact they had on the rest of the world while the passage to modernization was going on. The result of all this is that they really believe that economic assistance of, say, two dollars a head—the aid given to India—ought, in a decade, to be showing decisive results. The United States, starting in 1789 with a population of some 5 million in the emptiest and richest continent on the globe, still required about eighty years to move from small-scale farming to large-scale modern industry. In 1789 India already had over one hundred million people in an over-crowded continent and had a hundred and fifty years of colonial control to live through before its independent development could begin. Is it likely that the two decades since 1947 would have produced the decisive "breakthrough" to modernization? Even allowing for the preliminary development achieved under British rule, would not something nearer America's eight decades represent a more rational time scale? But how are people to make such judgements if they know virtually nothing of the history of the modernizing process and conceive themselves as springing, fully equipped and developed, into the arena of history?

This lack of historical judgement has a profound effect on another reason why support for economic assistance is tending to peter out. Faced with strains in the international monetary system—devaluation of sterling, pressure on the dollar, rampant speculation in gold— many people feel that the first need is to cut all "unnecessary" spending abroad and place foreign aid at the top of their priority list for the government's axe. But in 1929 when the last great collapse of the international economic system took place, it had been preceded by several years of decline in the economies of what are now called the developing countries. The prices for primary products had fallen steadily. Investment was slackening. Two thirds of the world's peoples were earning less. Hence they were buying less. The sharp contraction of their demand was one of the contributory causes to the general collapse of the international market in 1929 and 1930 when, in nine months, world trade fell by two thirds. Anyone aware of this historical background is bound to think twice about policies which, once again, might rip all strength of demand out of a large segment of the world market. But, then, how many know the history?

These problems of judgement and interpretation simply remind us that the bare facts do not always tell us what we ought to know. We need, too, a context within which to understand the facts. Again and again, the framework, not the bare event, determines our reactions. Take, for instance, the crucial question whether or not other people's misery should be the concern of prosperous citizens. At present we are debating the issue on a worldwide basis. But at one time the issue was still unsettled inside domestic society. To give a concrete example, from the 1860s onwards reformers had been warning the well-to-do classes in Britain that the new industrial cities were sinks of misery and disease. Then, in 1899, came the Boer War. The army recruits from these same cities proved everything the reformers had said. In York, for instance, a quarter of the recruits were completely "unfit" and another quarter barely reached the minimum standard. In the country at large, two out of five simply lacked the physical stamina for soldiering. At this point, however, the dominant groups took fright, and in order to restore the "imperial race"—as they were prone to call the British—they began to look for general reforms in health and welfare. Now in all this the misery and disease of the poor had not changed. The facts about them were well known. But the Boer War changed the context of influential thought. Within the framework of imperial interest, reforms that had been "inconceivable" a few years before became essential to survival. Such is the power of context to determine judgement.

The framework of our thinking also decides what weight we give to criticisms and attacks. There is not an educational system in the world that does not produce dropouts at every level—from the child in primary school out in the African bush who lasts no more than a year to the American student at a large university who lasts no longer. But the reaction to such failures is to try to improve the system. It certainly is not to say: "There you are. What did we tell you? Education has failed. Let us pack up the system and stop putting good money after bad." Similarly when the seventieth Starfighter falls out of the skies of Germany, no one suggests abandoning the defence effort. Astronauts lost on the launching pad do not cancel the space program. Criticism leads to cries of "abandon ship" only when the program itself is not securely rooted in public acceptance. If attacks are directed at what we know we must have, we try to improve it. We give up only what we do not believe we need.

Nowhere perhaps is this factor of context more decisive than in the way we look at the gap between rich nations and poor nations and decide whether our past efforts should be sustained or increased—or abandoned. We may know some of the facts—the plight of sick and hungry children in distant slums, the despair of their workless parents—but if neither history nor direct experience nor traditional policy give us a context for these facts of misery, we can think of them only in a disconnected and fragmentary way. If we took world assistance for granted as we do defence or education, the billions of dollars needed for policy would be found. But we do not have the same convictions. The facts themselves, however formidable, slop about in our minds outside any reliable frame of reference and produce neither understanding nor commitment.

So we need both information and a sense of context. What follows is an attempt to give some idea of where world wealth and world poverty fit into our general experience as citizens moving on towards the end of the twentieth century, steeped, many of us, in affluence, haunted, all of us, by the risk of nuclear destruction, yet hoping, nonetheless, that, in Winston Churchill's words, "God has not despaired of His children." And the first question clearly is whether our frame of reference need include other peoples at all. We have been more or less brought up to believe that the bonds of community, responsibility, and obligation run only to the frontiers. Should we extend our vision to include all the peoples of our planet? Or are all such phrases as "the family of man" simply the banal rhetoric of ceremonial occasions? This is where our enquiry must start for if there is no community, then subsidiary questions—about time scales and methods and reasonable expectations—are not of much concern. We can follow our instincts, do well for ourselves at home, let others look after themselves, and survive or succumb in the process.

Chapter Two

The Vision of Unity

Oₙₑ of the most
remarkable triumphs of vision over experience lies in
the fact that any kind of belief in the unity of mankind
ever contrived to emerge. The actual concrete experience of men encountering each other is of profound
and often unacceptable difference—in intelligence, in
shape, in skin-colour, in language, in culture. Collective encounters underline the differences even more
sharply. From the first tribe peering hungrily out of
the undergrowth at a neighbouring tribe's hunting
ground down to the latest, sophisticated act of mecha-
nised, air-supported aggression, the groups on the
other side of the frontiers have seemed as often as not

enemies rather than fellowmen—and enemies of whom all kinds of evil, including eating babies or boiling down cadavers for soap, have been happily believed.

Men have not lived as brothers. They have not treated each other as equals. They have recognised no common human family or destiny. They have repeatedly outraged the rights and dignity of fellowmen. War, conquest, enslavement, massacre, and pillage make up all too much of the wretched chronicle of human affairs. How, then, do we argue that these savage, murderous animals, hunting each other in cruel packs, are brothers, equal, responsible, and of incommensurable value and human worth? As the Duke of Wellington remarked to a stranger who addressed him as "Mr. Smith": "If you can believe that, you can believe anything."

And, indeed, it is a belief. It is an act of faith, and we can almost date the time of its appearance. One of the greatest, least studied, and most forgotten revolutions to overtake mankind occurred in the two or three millennia before the birth of Christ. At that time, all round the world, for reasons that are obscure and likely to remain so, a profound mutation took place in the way men looked at themselves, at each other, and at human destiny. Professor Christopher Dawson has described this worldwide change as the passage from an external religion of magic, propitiation, and sacrifice—the religion of tribal animism and the fertility cults—to an internal religion of purity of heart and observance of the moral law, to the philosophy of the great world religions—the Vedantas, Buddhism, Zoroastrianism, Confucianism, and Taoism, the Judaism of the Prophets, the Platonist vision of Greece. The Biblical phrase, "Obedience is better than sacrifice and to hearken than the fat of rams," is one way of describing this sense that "true religion and undefiled" has nothing to do with trying to manipulate unknown forces—or gods—by fetish and ritual. At this level, religion is almost a nursery affair of wants and claims and wish fulfilment. Rather is religion concerned with the depths of man's being in which he is or is not capable of love, fortitude, generosity, and truth—the disciplines which, in this new vision, alone make him truly human.

But at this level of depth, men encounter each other not as strangers but as other selves. On the surface lie all the differences—of race and nation and culture and creed. At heart, men share a common human substance—in the foreknowledge of death, in dependence and vulnerability, the need for love, the need for respect, the need for spontaneity, the need for some purpose in their existence. To recognise and cherish this common nature in another man is the essence of that much abused word, love. A religion of the heart or spirit turns men away from the inessentials and makes them capable of the great command of all the world religions—to love one's neighbour as oneself.

But of all the religious systems which arose from the new inward sense of the moral law, none attained the intensity of belief in man that we find in the Judeo-Christian tradition of our own Western society. While, all around, the tribes and empires of the Middle East worshipped their totems and their fertility goddesses and their local deities, the Jewish tribe astonishingly ascribed to their God the lordship of the entire human race. They might be His chosen people but they were only instruments in a worldwide purpose, a tool among the nations in the hands of a God Who was God over all the nations, the single God of all created things, common Father of the single brotherhood of all mankind.

It is difficult to believe that any gap in history has ever equalled the gap between soaring idea and constrained reality in this Jewish vision. While their leaders were captive in Babylon, their land occupied, and their holy city desolate, this tiny tribe sat in chains by the alien waters and proclaimed their God the Lord of everything and their destiny the key to the future of all humanity. And the odd thing is, they were perfectly right. Nothing in our catastrophic modern world would be conceivable without the Jewish vision of God's purpose unfolding progressively in time through the instrumentality of men who do His will. In its Christian version, it is the philosophical foundation of the Western world. In its Marxist version, it is the basis of the secular vision of world Communism.

In Christianity the unity and brotherhood of man find their most profound and indeed mysterious affirmation. For Christ is the Son of Man. He is the first born of a new humanity, a Second Adam, and this new race will share a unity as close as branches of a vine or

members of a body. The phrases used to describe this
new community suggest a unity far closer than that of
brotherly good will, respect, and common purpose
among men. The suggestion is of a union more profound even than the unity of a family. All mankind is
called to this union. There are no distinctions—"neither Jew nor Gentile, male nor female, slave nor
free"—all are members one of another in a unity which
in some inexplicable fashion mirrors the indissoluble
union of our physical being. It is virtually impossible
to push the concept of human unity further than this.

Then the Christians took this vision of unity out into
a world as obstinately distant and divided as ever. The
man who went from Jerusalem to Jericho and fell
among thieves went on a mule, and eighteen hundred
years later the Founding Fathers riding to Philadel-
phia went no quicker. The Apostle Paul sailing round
the Eastern Mediterranean found his movements as
much restricted by wind and tide as did the Jesuit missionaries going out to India in the sixteenth century.
The world of vast distance and vaster ignorance, of
myths of Prester John and the Grand Cham of Tartary,
of rumoured gold and distant Utopias continued for
another millennium and a half after the death of Christ.
The Christian idea of the unity, equality, and brotherhood of all mankind remained like a hidden seed in the
hard soil of limited transport, local sovereignty, feudal
structures, and tribal division. The brotherhood of all
mankind was hardly a compelling concept to people
who never left their own village—and only the excep-

tional Christians ever practised much brotherhood even there. But the seed remained and with it the lurking possibility that at some point a harrow would pass over the earth and release that seed's potential and explosive force.

Today, the harrow has passed. It is a familiar one—the harrow of revolutionary scientific invention and technology. In two short centuries, the world of distance and strangeness has been totally abolished. Messages and voices, bouncing off space satellites, give mankind instant communication and joint vision. The whole world watched the funeral of President Kennedy as it happened—as though all humanity were present at a universal wake. Physical space is vanishing. The man in the jet plane circles the globe in twenty-eight hours, the man in the spaceship circles it in as many minutes and sees a dozen sunrises and sunsets in the span of a normal day and night. And soon the astronauts speeding to Mars will look back and see Earth no larger than a spaceship voyaging among interplanetary distances and carrying a single crew—the human race.

This analogy is not simply visual. On any journey among the planets, the astronauts' survival depends totally upon the invulnerability of the spaceship. Shatter this shell, this cover, this capsule of security and the whole crew perishes out in interstellar space. But atomic annihilation is a possibility facing our planet. And once it is accomplished, there will be no other place in all infinity where men can go for refuge.

Thus the Christian vision of a humanity made one in the organic unity of a terrestrial family is no longer a total fantasy. In physical, scientific, and technological terms, the facts of unity are now more compelling than the facts of distance—not least in the final frightening possibility of total and united involvement in atomic extinction.

Moreover, man's union in a single system is not simply physical and technical. To an increasing extent, the way in which he earns his daily bread is taking on the extra dimension of a planetary context. Steadily from the sixteenth century onwards—but with a vertiginous rate of acceleration after the invention of the steamship in the nineteenth century—the world has been transformed into a dense cocoon of investment and commerce. The lines of finance and trade wrap us round and round; and with each new discovery, each new local development, each new dramatic change in technique, new lines spin out, making the cocoon more inextricable and dense. At present, for instance, air freight across the Atlantic is increasing by some 30 per cent a year. Here the new lines are spun at jet speed and the enmeshing goes forward with the vigor of an automatic loom.

It is difficult to exaggerate the interdependence of this new worldwide economy. If Canada and the United States could not produce a vast surplus of grain, millions of people in Russia and China and India would go hungry. If Western children lost their taste for chocolate, the farmers of Ghana and Nigeria would lose a large part of their cash income. If everyone in America drank an extra cup of coffee every day, it could mean a sharp reinvigoration of the Brazilian economy. Between 1952 and 1962, all the investment going into Latin America was offset by the fall in world prices for Latin America's major exports. Nowhere perhaps is interdependence more striking than in this field of the financing of international trade. The ability of the world to maintain its vast trading system for the last decade has depended upon the willingness of the United States to pump out more dollars into the world than it brings back by way of sales and earnings—and on the willingness of the major traders in Europe to look on dollars as being "as good as gold." If the American deficit were to vanish, overnight the whole world trading system would be short of essential working capital and would have either to invent an alternative or cut its transactions sharply back.

Such instances of interdependence can be multiplied from every corner of the globe. Today it is virtually true to say that the moment an economy moves out of subsistence agriculture where farmers simply produce food for themselves and their families, it is insensibly caught up in a web of economic activities spreading across every ocean and every continent. The decision to modernize today is the equivalent of the decision to enter the worldwide economy.

These new interdependences of production and commerce spring from a much deeper change—the steady movement of all mankind away from pre-technological methods of working and producing and on into the modern scientific and technical community. This is a secular change, comparable to the shift from hunting to settled agriculture. Just as, over the millennia, the areas where people rely wholly on hunting, fishing, and food-gathering have shrunk to a few tiny patches of desert or rain forest, so today a new kind of scientific method and technological apparatus is gradually pressing back the limits of the pre-technological society. And the hallmark of the new economies is precisely their ability to create wealth, their incomparable capacity to enhance man's power to make nature yield him a living.

The effort is not new—only the success. For thousands and thousands of years—in fact ever since the first tribe used the first axe to clear a corner of the forest—it has been men's chief preoccupation with the physical world. First they hunted and gathered berries, simply taking what nature offered. Then they copied the seeding of nature and planted the grain they could later gather. Then, in some areas, they moved from control of the grain to control of the soil. Vast works of irrigation grew up in the great river valleys and were the basis of the first post-tribal societies and civilizations. And these works of water control stimulated measurement—of land for dykes and flooding, of the heavens for the ebb and flow of the seasons. Measurement, revealing nature's uniformities, was precursor to the fundamental tool of rational control over the material environment—mathematics. This the

Chaldeans and Egyptians and Greeks together had managed to invent well before the beginning of the Christian era.

But for another two millennia, the tool was little used. It remained an intellectual pursuit, a source of contemplation, a delight and wonder to the philosophers. It was only gradually, from the time of the Renaissance onwards, in one corner of the globe—Western Europe—that men began to realize, in the wake of Leonardo da Vinci, that mathematics also offered the secret to mechanics, to the practical and critical control of energy for human purposes. Until the Newcomen engine, first put to work in 1704—and now sitting intact in the Ford museum at Dearborn—all energy had been natural energy, animal power, wind power, the power of the tides, the heat of charcoal. All these had been applied to human needs. The smelting of iron and copper goes back into the mists of legend and myth. Mariners went round the world under sail and discovered all the continents. But the Newcomen engine, using the energy of steam under pressure to pump out a mine, produced the first "invented" energy and opened wide the door to the application of increasing power to all human activities. It began with relatively simple substitutions—machines to reinforce and replace the skill of hands and weight of bodies. It moved on, through increasingly sophisticated forms of energy—electricity, nuclear power—to reinforce and replace with computers much of the work of the human mind. And in all these substitutions the result

was more output for less effort and input—what Buck-
minster Fuller calls "the more for less"—a growing
store of wealth, a growing capacity to control and enhance man's natural environment, a growing ability to
compel nature to yield higher and more dynamic living
standards to those in command of the new instruments.

Today the differences between the affluence of one
fifth of humanity and the aspirations of all the rest are
determined by their place on the ladder of modernization. The process is a single one, embracing the whole
planet. One fifth of humanity have reached standards
of wealth and competence which ensure their continu-
ance. The others have not and this is the cause of the
gap between them. If the lopsidedness is to be re-
duced—between the 20 per cent with 80 per cent of
the resources and the 80 per cent with 20—the first
need is to accelerate the processes of modernization
and to apply to the poorer nations those methods and
strategies which have proven themselves among the
affluent. So the preliminary issue is to know what are
these processes.

Chapter Three

Ways to Wealth

THE SHORT ANSWER to the problem of devising a strategy for growth is to say that the sources of modern wealth lie in the building up of savings (or capital), in scientific invention, in advancing technology and trained and sophisticated minds. Wherever economies have acquired these instruments of wealth, they become rich and grow richer, even though they may, like Denmark, lack most of the more notable physical resources such as oil or coal or iron ore or even good soil. Economies which have not yet fashioned the instruments of modernization are poor even though, like Indonesia, they may be fantastically well-endowed.

(33)

It is a fact of history that the societies which first made the breakthrough to the modern technological economy happened to lie round the North Atlantic; and today, after nearly two hundred years of chequered growth, they are richer than anyone could have foreseen, even a couple of decades ago. And since scientific discovery has a built-in principle of acceleration—the more you know, the larger the base from which you can attack the still unknown—it is at least possible that the creation of further wealth will accelerate in the same way.

But simply to say that the North Atlantic powers are richer because they have modernized their economies really tells us almost nothing about our interdependent world order. It gives us no idea of how the transformation occurred, or whether other peoples can accomplish it. It gives us no context within which to judge the vast and increasing distance between rich and poor societies. It gives us no clue at all to possible means of lessening the gap. For instance, we could say—and quite a lot of people do say—that certain nations or peoples or races are quite incapable of producing the intellectual vigour and the national discipline needed to transform their economy and so are destined to remain feckless, improvident, and poor. The top candidates for this irredeemable status vary. A century ago, all Asians were believed to be industrially incompetent, until Japan upset the old images. Latins were supposed by Anglo-Saxons to be hopelessly stagnant and feudal until Italy began to produce its postwar

(34)

economic "miracle" and Spain launched itself towards effective modernization. Today, no doubt, Laotians vie with Congolese for a supposed preeminence in incapacity. Tomorrow there will be different candidates and by then some of the present laggards may well have begun to catch up while others may have fallen behind. The history of technological change so far should make us wary of all talk of innate and immutable barriers to economic change. The important point is how the transformations have been made, not whether skin colour or social psyche or national tradition unfits people to change at all.

Perhaps the best way, in shorthand, to describe the changes which lead to modern material abundance is to look at them occurring in two pioneer countries —both small, both islands, neither of them too well endowed in natural resources, neither in a sense the obvious candidates for modern economies. Yet Britain was the world's pioneer in modernization and Japan the first innovator in Asia. At the same time, they are so far apart—in history, in culture, in social experience—that what they have in common is likely to be typical not of their own community only but of the processes—and the problems—of modernization itself. We can pick out five factors, all crucial, and make the guess that in any community where these are lacking, the modernization of the economy is unlikely to occur.

The first is political—the existence of a coherent and purposeful national sense. In fact, it is unlikely that the whole transformation of society which modernization involves can be accomplished without a sustained act of collective will. Britain had forged its nationhood in hot commercial competition with other maritime powers in Europe who were becoming nations under the same pressures. From the sixteenth century onwards, British merchants competing with Holland and France for the spice trade in Asia or with Spain and Portugal for the slave trade in Africa became aware of their identity as national traders and usually had state support in setting up the monopolies which, they felt, were alone strong enough to guard them against both the competition of other nations and the appalling physical risks of cockle-shell boats, unknown oceans, and scurvy-ridden crews.

This stimulus to the idea of a national market, bounded in Britain's case by the natural boundaries of the sea, did far more than control the organization of foreign trade. It began to shape an economic unit which was both wide enough to transcend the old limited subsistence economy of villages and small market towns, yet at the same time compact enough to avoid the uncertain administration and local tolls, octroi, internal barriers, and general disorders and vagaries of large imperial units such as the Holy Roman Empire or imperial China.

Japan achieved its sense of nationhood by excluding all European traders from the sixteenth to the nineteenth centuries. Then, when Western pressure became irresistible after 1850, the country was sufficiently united and coherently governed first to bend to

Western demands for trading privileges and then to transform the Japanese economy speedily enough to hold the foreigners off.

It is significant that at that same time China proved too big and unwieldy to make the transition by its own decisions and lapsed into a century of anarchy and exploitation by outside interests. This, then, is the first factor—an independent government exercising undoubted national authority over an area large enough, yet compact enough, to become a functioning market.

The second point is intellectual—the training of minds in modern science, technology, and rational administration. It was in Britain that men of education first turned, massively, to the study of the natural sciences, in some measure as a revulsion against the theology and metaphysics which had divided them so bitterly in the long struggles over religion. All through Britain in the eighteenth century, every kind of man—from dukes to artisans—dabbled in scientific experiment. Watt's homely teakettle launched mankind on the age of steam. At the same time, revivalist religion—the Methodists, the Evangelicals—helped to teach reading, the Bible, and self-improvement to the mass of the people.

These changes were critical. The energy unlocked in steam, working through new processes and machines invented by a multitude of ingenious minds, trebled, quadrupled, centupled man's ability to produce goods. The flood of invention had started and has not ceased in two hundred years. Today when impulses on earth set the cameras which photograph the dark side of the moon or the flick of a switch can release a thousand times the power that annihilated Hiroshima, the flood is a cataract, a deluge, inundating every human activity and demanding, in every field of work, the cooperation of trained minds and sophisticated skills.

The Japanese cannot be counted pioneers in the British sense. At first, as is well known, they copied their technology from the more developed West. But they were innovators in realizing, with singleminded clarity, that the technical skills must be learnt and that the Japanese people would need universal literacy. Moreover, by the time their economic revolution had come of age, they, too, began to innovate themselves, nowhere perhaps more successfully than in the boldness and complexity of their postwar policies of economic management and foreign trade.

With a coherent will to change and some understanding of the needed technical instruments—power, machines, skilled workers—the modernizing community confronts a third issue: the central economic issue of its ability to produce savings. The secret of the new techniques is, as we have noticed, that they give a far bigger return for the same inputs of energy and materials. But they do not give the bigger return at once. In a sense, saving is the price paid for waiting. A spring gives water at once. A well takes a little time to dig, though it then gives a larger supply; meantime the diggers must eat and drink and someone must pay them—in other words, the man who decides to have a well dug must have money put by to cover the costs. He must have savings. A complicated well has to be manufactured in a factory, transported, and installed. The wait and the cost are greater still. So is the final output. A huge dam, providing irrigation and power, takes a decade to build, involves thousands of men and thousands of subsidiary operations, all of which must be financed before any increased output comes from the system. So savings must be made to cover the costs of waiting and one of the most intricate decisions on economic planning is to get the time cycles of different investments worked out so that the schemes with quick returns come in in time to finance the larger projects whose ultimate productivity may be much higher but is much slower to achieve. And one of the most usual errors is, often for prestige's sake or for conspicuous nation-building, to invest in the largest and most monumental works, disregarding the cost in resources for daily living while the people have to wait out, with tightened belts, the construction of "their" High Dam.

But however sensible the timetable of development, there is no way in the short run of making it cheap. A simple agricultural economy with some foreign trade, some artisan manufacture and, perhaps, some mining is the usual starting point. Britain was more sophisticated than most in the early stages. Its foreign trade had helped to stimulate banking, insurance, and fiscal management generally, also to build up a variety of pre-mechanical industries—iron smelting from charcoal, seacoal, woollens. Yet it was only in the eighteenth century that banking spread to the whole country, tapping new savings in the provinces. Only in the eighteenth century did the turnpikes begin to put in a road system in which industrial goods were not lost in the mud. The amount of saving—or capital—needed to mechanize the textile industry, introduce rotation and manuring to the farmers, house the workers streaming into Manchester and the wool towns, build roads and canals, construct new ports, set up mechanics institutes, and bear the loss of the experimental failures went far beyond the accumulated capital of even dukes, country gentlemen, bankers, and nabobs from the new British conquests in India. (The plundering of Bengal brought in a handsome increment of bullion.) Everyone had to save—"everyone" included workers who had virtually no margin on which to do so. The misery of the new industrial cities, horrifyingly described in Dickens's *Little Dorrit* or *Hard Times,* sprang from the iron need to take all the surplus produced by the new machines and divert it from the poor, who would have consumed it, to the rich who, having enough, reinvested it. Indeed, if they had not done so, the economy would have ceased to grow.

In Japan, this same ruthless process of "primitive accumulation" was carried on at first largely by a determined government acting against the clock—the clock of Western demands and encroachments. But the impact was a little softened by the wholesale Japanese land reforms of the 1870s which gave the land to the peasant and compensated the landlords in industrial bonds. The farmer, freed from feudal dues, increased his output three times over. Even while paying two thirds of the surplus to the government for development, he still was better off, and he provided a market for the new light industrial goods—bicycles, sewing machines. The poor were still poor, and the government and the big clans controlled the investment. But sound agrarian policies cushioned the harshness of early saving.

It did more. It pointed to a fifth condition of modernization—the primacy of agriculture. The phrase "industrial revolution" darkens counsel. In effect, everything has to be revolutionized, not least farming. Farming is always the major economic activity at the beginning of modernization. If it does not become more productive, from where are savings to come, short of starving the people? The British landowners had in fact concentrated and capitalized their farms before industrialization began, and four-crop rotation and winter feed were among the revolutions which permitted the new urban workers to be fed. Stalin's neglect of agriculture still holds Russia back. India's delay in giving priority to fertilizer and small irrigation has jeopardised its Plans. And wherever stagnant feudal land-ownership persists—as in much of Latin America—industrialization is crippled for lack of a rural market. "Invest in farming" should be inscribed above every planner's desk.

As for the process which is popularly supposed to

determine everything—industrialization—Britain and Japan both point to the same factors, that consumer goods such as textiles and household requirements are a logical place to begin and that where you go from there will be determined by your own pattern of resources and your ability to trade abroad. Britain, endowed with coal and iron ore and a damp climate, based its early prosperity on selling textiles and machinery. Japan, endowed chiefly with silkworms and mulberry bushes, based its foreign trade on silk. But Australia has grown rich on wool, Denmark on bacon, New Zealand on lamb. It is the efficiency that counts, not the content—which varies from country to country, according to minerals, rainfall, soil, or forests. These are the variables. But the structure of modernization, from Asia to Europe and back again, stands on the same universal foundations—a national purpose and market, intellectual vigour, savings, reformed agriculture, and appropriate industrialization. And the processes of modernization, involving as they do changes in every sector of a nation's life, are not accomplished in less than half a century and in many cases—notably that of France—spread nearer to a hundred years.

The five critical points of change can also be described as the necessary engines for sustained growth. Without them an economy will not leave the ground. But they do not of themselves guarantee a safe journey. The machine has to "take off." It must also stay air-borne and, in the last hundred and fifty years or so of modernization, the experiment has shown alarming tendencies to lose height periodically—for some years after 1929 it even lay flat on the ground. And it is of more than simple historical interest to notice that many of the men who first tried to analyse the new economy in the early part of the nineteenth century were very doubtful whether the machine would work at all.

They believed the central energy for the whole process lay in men's ability to make profits. Profits simply expressed the fact that "the more for less" was taking place. If at the end of an industrial or agricultural investment the entrepreneur was not getting more out of the process than he put in, then clearly he was creating no new resources and providing no surplus for further investment in further growth. Connecting "profits" with private greed has rather obscured this point. Every successful enterprise, public or private, must make a profit. Otherwise, it is likely to be making a loss and actually decreasing the flow of wealth. The Communists have realized this, and profits are no longer a dirty word in Moscow.

But many of the early economists thought profits could not be sustained. They had worries on the side of supply and worries on the side of demand. Once the best land and the most easily available minerals and the most intelligent workers had been drawn into the productive process, might not the next lot of resources be so much more inefficient and hence expensive that rising costs would squeeze out profits and so bring fur-

(43)

ther investment to an end? On the side of demand, once the reasonably wealthy people had been satisfied, where could a larger market be found? If you paid workers higher wages, costs would go up and the profit squeeze would again bring expansion to an end. In any case, if you paid them anything more than the wages needed to keep themselves alive and reproduce themselves, they simply had more children (*proles*—hence "proletarians") and brought themselves back to the old dead level of poverty. So between rising costs and a static market, the new system's prospects for sustained growth looked grim indeed.

Marx made them grimmer by adding the political gloss that the selfish rich would not in any case share wealth more widely. Their absolute control over private property channelled all the profits and the capital gains into their own pockets, and they were, he argued, much too concerned with their own self-interest to distribute their prosperity more generously. They would rather see the whole system break down and, since they ran the system, ultimate disaster must follow.

When the early economists—including Marx—made their analysis, it did not lack foundation. For the first five decades of the nineteenth century, the British workers gained very little from the new machines. The surplus did go back to the rich who reinvested it. The poor remained abjectly poor. The business cycle did bump up and down as costs squeezed out profits and expansion stopped until demand picked up again. After 1870, the check to growth lasted nearly two decades. And in countries in which the feudal structure of society remained largely unchanged—Russia, Southern Europe, Latin America—incipient industrialization was strangled by lack of markets since the mass of people in the countryside had no access to the new wealth and went on miserably sharecropping or paying rack rents—a condition which effectively inhibits the growth of the market and hence of modernization in some areas even today.

Yet in the North Atlantic area the gloomy prophecies have been largely disproved, and the reasons go far to explain its massive prosperity. On the side of supply, two unforeseen changes contradicted the fears of the early economists. The picture of marginal land being brought in at great cost to feed a rising population faded before massive investment in new resources overseas. British and then European and American capital was speedily exported to other continents, there to invest in vast new sources of supply—wheat, beef, coffee—from the New World, oil palms and cocoa from West Africa, tea and jute and cotton in Asia, minerals everywhere. These were the decades when Western investment and trade drove forward all round the world, opening up farms and mines and plantations, uprooting migrant workers—Chinese, Negroes, East Indians—to work in them and, in the process, bringing the most distant lands and the most ignorant peoples into the intricate and widening web of a new global economy.

The second change was even more momentous—the

wholly unexpected productivity of the new techniques. Energy multiplied until enough was available to blow up the planet. Fertilizers and hybrids increased a thousandfold mankind's potential supply of food. New geological instruments vastly increased the areas of known mineral reserves while new processes used them infinitely more efficiently. With such a flood of new materials and new inventions, productivity, the ability to produce more for less, grew steadily, leaving a margin for both profits and wages to increase together. The limits are still there—as we know from our current pressure of costs on profits—but they can accommodate weekly wages of 200 dollars and more and are thus inconceivably wider than a Ricardo or a Malthus ever dreamt of in their wildest imaginings.

The changes on the side of demand have been even more fateful. Marx believed the workers would not get a larger share of the new wealth because the rich ran the government and would resist any change. But in Britain and America—and increasingly in Europe—the poor acquired the vote, and became the majority; they enjoyed civil rights and formed trade unions. They were thus in a position to redress the balance, bargaining for higher wages and voting funds for education, health, and urban improvement out of the taxes increasingly paid by the wealthy. Nor were the rich uniformly unenlightened. Christians denounced the evils of uncontrolled exploitation. Little by little, management began to realize the advantage of contented, well-educated workers. Moderate socialists appealed for a

(46)

more creative view of government responsibility. The Soviet Union proved that, whatever central direction of the economy might not do, it could vastly accelerate early growth. Thus pressure from the poor, from educated opinion, from experience, from the enlightenment of rulers conspired to bring about a new view of the responsibilities of Government. It would not simply confine itself to law and order in the old sense. It acquired the positive task of maintaining economic health and this has increasingly meant, since the last war, the maintenance of enough monetary demand in the economy to employ all the nation's resources and workers and to encourage further investment and further growth.

This new technique of "demand management" may not yet be fully mastered or understood. But the world is now in its third postwar decade without a major recession. Between 1919 and 1939, there were three, one of them devastating. Moreover, America and Europe together have, since the beginning of the sixties, achieved rates of growth well over 3 per cent a year —in Japan anything less than 7 per cent is looked on as a recession. Such increases explain their ability, all of them together, to add each year about $60,000 million to their vast, existing wealth.

(47)

Chapter Four

The Latecomers

THE Atlantic Powers have developed not only themselves in the last two centuries. They are very largely responsible for the start of modernization everywhere else. Atlantic trade and investment first carried the new ideas and new techniques around the world. And this first impact has helped to determine the possibilities and obstructions in the path of development in other lands. True, the developing continents below the Tropic of Cancer had certain common characteristics. They included the Tropics, with leached soils, unmanageable rainfall, and millennia of malarial infection. They were little endowed with coal in the age of steam. Only a few areas had oil in the age of the internal combustion engine—and the oil lay mainly under sand, not under fertile land as in Texas or Alberta. But poverty is increasingly a reflection of the lack of technical resourcefulness. In developing as in developed lands, the balance of resources is less important than the achievement of modernization.

Here the starting point, under the stimulus of Atlantic trade and investment, was extremely haphazard and no one really quite intended what actually came about. However, states must take the consequences of what they do, even if the outcome is accidental. The Atlantic peoples should remember that the problems confronting the developing nations take the form they show today largely as a result of an overwhelming Atlantic impact, lasting over two or three centuries, on the rest of mankind.

Two forces drove on the peoples of Western Europe—nationalism and the desire to trade or, as a sterner critic might put it, pride and cupidity. From the sixteenth to the twentieth century, these two vast drives brought the whole planet under Western control. Spaniards and Portuguese went out to Latin America to get the gold and stayed to take the land. British and French settlers occupied North America, the British later pushing on to Australia and New Zealand and to all the temperate lands of Africa not already preempted by Boers or Portuguese. Some 40 million of Africa's own inhabitants were in turn hunted, killed, or enslaved and the survivors sent in floating charnal houses to the Americas, there to make up for local inhabitants who were either decimated by the European invasions or were too small or too untameable for concentrated work. In the seventeenth and eighteenth centuries, all Europe's maritime powers tried to monopolize the fabulous trade in spices, silks, and precious metals with the then still wealthy continent of Asia. In the course of it, they took over local countries in order to establish monopolies and keep each other out. Indonesia fell to Holland, India to Britain, South East Asia—later—to France. Once gold had been discovered in South Africa in the 1870s, a similar process partitioned the whole African continent between most of the same European powers—with Holland subtracted and Belgium and Germany added. As in Asia, the direct intention was in the main not to colonize, only to trade, invest, and keep other nations out. But the outcome was colonization and direct control.

This Western impact introduced all the continents to the ideas and possibilities of the modern scientific and technological society. We cannot say whether they could themselves have invented comparable opportunities. History is irreversible and since the Western nations were the pioneers, no one can say whether other nations could have taken their place. Yet if Europeans become excessively arrogant about their contributions to the modern age, one can only remind them that some of the most essential tools of their advance—the alphabet, for instance, and mathematics—were first evolved in Middle Eastern societies and that some of the communities they found in Asia were widely be-

(51)

lieved, as late as the eighteenth century, to have far surpassed the West in wealth and wisdom. That the Chinese used gunpowder for firecrackers, not war, does not necessarily prove any lack of technical inventiveness. On the contrary, if Western technology finally blows up the world, it can hardly be reckoned a progressive force.

Yet the Western powers have provided a stream of innovating ideas and inventions. Their colonial systems did introduce Asia and Africa and, to some extent, Latin America to the Pandora's box of modernity. They can claim—without proof but equally without refutation—that the ex-colonial peoples of the developing world could not have reached the modern threshold so quickly without them. Westerners, no doubt, will tend to remember all that has been beneficent in the process—dedicated missionaries, the beginnings of literacy and health, the new crops and methods, law and order, tribal peace, the devoted district officers, the orderly transfer, in most areas, to independent government. The peoples themselves will have more divided memories, recalling, too, subjection, bewilderment, racial humiliation, the sense of serving others' purposes without understanding them, and at last an independence for which technically they were often ill-prepared. Perhaps it is still too soon to strike a balance sheet. But today in the immediate aftermath of worldwide Western control, one can at least say that the colonial inheritance, along with its advantages, has created some tough obstacles to the processes of speedy modernization.

The typical ex-colony is a country in which changes are only partial. Western investment has usually come in to develop a raw material in demand in European or American markets. Perhaps a mine provides this export, perhaps a plantation. If local labour falls short, Chinese or Indians or Africans may be shipped in—as they have been throughout the Caribbean or in Fiji or South East Asia—to do the unskilled work. The mineral or foodstuff is then exported to Atlantic markets, and this requires modern railways, roads, and ports —virtually all the big cities in the developing world are seaports, and the lines of communication run down to them almost like drains. But this development of trade does not imply processing the raw materials. Atlantic tariffs are so arranged that there are few obstacles to the entry of unworked materials. Processed goods have higher and higher obstacles to jump as they become more worked up and completed. This bias lessens the developing lands' ability to export manufactured goods—in fact they provide less than 5 per cent of the world's trade in manufactures.

The export sector also requires only a few local skills—clerks, tally men, stevedores. And it does not set in motion very much other local development, for little of the capital created in the restricted exporting process spills over into the rest of the economy. The chief fallout is ideas and ambitions and, sooner or later, the resentment of local peoples seeing, but not sharing in, the opportunities of modernization.

It is not difficult to see the effect of this impact on the five fundamental changes needed for modernization. First of all, national will—under a colonial government, nationalism has been both stimulated and suppressed. Local people were assumed—not always wrongly—to be unready for self government in modern conditions and, in some systems, given no chance to learn. The *reductio ad absurdum* of this process could be seen in the Congo where for decades no elective government was introduced, not even for municipalities. Then, after only some eighteen months of chaotic party politics, the country took a headlong plunge into independence. In India, on the contrary, where local voting was introduced fifty years and more before independence, a coherent national political system could emerge. But in many ex-colonies, the vehemence of national feeling is only equalled by its inexperience, and in Africa, in particular, very few of the new nation-states have territory or resources enough to form a coherent market.

Next, literacy—in most of the ex-colonial worlds the demands of the export sectors for educated people were, as we have noticed, very small. Parents might educate their children in mission schools or abroad but governments did not aim at general literacy. Usually, less than a quarter of the people had any primary education, less than 2 per cent had been to secondary school, and only a small elite had ever attended a university—the figure for the Congo was 30 graduates for 14 million people. Even where, as in India or Latin America, there is a cultural tradition of great brilliance, modern skills—in engineering, in science, in agriculture—are still scarce and intermediate leadership at the level of foreman and skilled technician requires very rapid expansion.

Next, savings—the typical colonial impact did not generate local savings. The investment was provided by business firms in Europe and America, and the profits and capital gains flowed back to the North Atlantic. The sales organizations, transport, banking, and insurance required for international commerce were, and still are, largely controlled by Western business. Senior salaries tended to be paid to Westerners and in part repatriated. Then any spare local purchasing power left over was mopped up through the sale by large or small expatriate concerns of consumer goods manufactured in the West. And to complete the cycle of disadvantage, over long periods the prices paid for unprocessed primary materials have tended to fluctuate widely—in the fifties all capital going into Latin America was cancelled by the fall in primary prices —whereas the price of manufactured goods has steadily gone up. From this circuit, not unnaturally, almost no savings spilled over into the local economy. The French coined a phrase for it—*l'économie de traite*—the milch cow economy. Only rarely, as round Bombay or in Minas Geraes, did local diversification begin.

For without savings, how could the fourth and fifth point be achieved? To transform traditional farming requires capital. So does any form of local industrialization. Outside the plantations, foreign investors were not interested in food farming. Colonial administrators tended to leave local subsistence customs—tribal or feudal—unchanged. Feudal landowners did not reform themselves. As for industry, few colonial governments were intent on encouraging manufactures which competed with those of the mother country. India could not set up a tariff to assist local textiles until 1920. To compare its sluggish industrial growth with Japan's bounding expansion is telling evidence of the inhibitions imposed by colonial control.

Thus on every count one can risk the generalization that a century of more or less colonial control produced in the developing continents a condition of semi-modernization in which the export sectors and their auxiliary services, transport, markets, and cities had entered the modern technical world, had drawn in a section of the population, and had broadcast modern ideas and ambitions much more widely. But the bulk of the people remained in unchanged stagnation and poverty.

This was the inheritance. In the decade or so that has followed the ending of the colonial system, new governments have started to experience the full contradictions and difficulties of this inheritance. We are beginning to see that while the basic preconditions of modernization—political will, literacy, savings, modern farming, industry—have not changed, it is very much more difficult to modernize today than it was a hundred years ago. There are advantages—the existence of technologies and techniques which do not need to be reinvented, an existing world economy into which new economies can plug themselves. But the difficulties tend in the short run to offset these gains. Each of them helps to explain why no developing country today can be expected to leap into modernization within the time limit set by Western impatience and Western ignorance.

Once more, we come back to the problem of context. Reasonable expectations for growth and change in the developing world can only be based upon the facts. But how can such judgement be made if the tough realities are ignored? Nothing sensible can be said about the prospects of modernization in the rest of the world unless four or five basic contradictions, all bred of *this* century's conditions, are borne in mind.

1) *The disproportion between the production of food and of people:* As we have seen, the colonial and semi-colonial economies of the "developing South" did not, in the main, reform agriculture outside production for export. In general, food production remained in the subsistence sector. In Africa it was communal. In many parts of Latin America, landless peasants lived on the fringes of under-utilized great estates. In Asia, tiny farms, in a harsh network of landlord-tenant, usurer-debtor relationships, covered the land. All produced overwhelmingly for subsistence and little for the market. But the years of relative peace under colonial rule and the beginnings of public health set in motion the first phase of the "population explosion." It soon had disastrous consequences in Asia since China and India entered modern times with already densely pop-

(57)

ulated countrysides. In India, the decline in per capita nourishment had set in by the end of the nineteenth century. In the twentieth, war-torn pre-Communist China faced catastrophic shortages.

Since the war, both countries have reversed the stagnation in farm output. Indian food supplies have increased by 3 per cent a year, apart from monsoon failures. China's figures give great leaps backwards and forwards but the evidence suggests at least an average of 3 to 4 per cent. However, population growth, at 2.7 per cent or higher, wipes out these gains and threatens worse pressure. India is growing by nearly 13 million a year, China possibly by more. Together they will help to boost Asia's population from just under 2 billion today to 4.4 billion by the year 2000. Before the last war, Asia could still export food—about 2 million tons of grain a year in the 1930s. In 1960, it had to import 16 million. In the famine year of 1966, the figure rose to 30 million. The astounding productivity of North American agriculture suggests that even a deficit twice as large as this could be met from outside resources. But how would the poor continents pay for such vast transfers? And could they be sure of receiving them as gifts?

In Africa and Latin America, the explosion has begun against the background of a much emptier countryside. Both continents can accommodate the three-fold increase which will bring Africa to 800 million and Latin America to 700 million by the year 2000. But they cannot do so with present methods of producing food. Latin America was an exporter of grain—an average of 9 million tons a year in the 1930s. The exports have virtually ceased in the sixties. Africa has turned a modest prewar export surplus into an average of 2 million tons of imports. Once again, future imports on a rising scale into both continents raise the agonizing issue of how the procurement of so much food is to be financed.

Neither North America nor Europe experienced these pressures during their own period of modernization. Agriculture was transformed and industry introduced before the spurt in population took hold. In fact, Britain could hardly have expanded its economy if the birth rate had not shot up in the early nineteenth century. The United States, beginning its independent life with only some 5 million people, had to import as well as produce millions of workers to undertake the opening of a vast empty continent. By the time technology demanded fewer raw "hands" and better trained skills in its labor force, population in both countries had begun to stabilize. By the luck of history, the Atlantic powers got the ratio of supplies to consumers about right. The developing world is swamped with would-be consumers before the supplies are even in sight.

2) *The disproportion between urban growth and urban employment:* In the Atlantic world, cities grew up together with the industries which enticed thousands of migrants to come in from the country. Virtually only London and Paris had more than a million inhabitants in the 1780s. America had nothing above

New York's 50,000. The vast growth of cities accompanied the vast growth of job-producing industry and food-producing agriculture.

In the developing world, thanks to the colonial patterns of trade, vast cities came into being to serve the export trade long before general modernization really began. Rio, Buenos Aires, Caracas, Lagos, Dakar, Alexandria, Beirut, Bombay, Calcutta, Singapore, Shanghai—all round the world these trading ports and entrepôt centers drew in millions of people to the bright lights and supposed opportunities. Foreign business set up its enterprises there and increased the pull. But out in the hinterland, stagnant agriculture could not hold its young men or feed the cities. This imbalance has grown worse. Five thousand migrants come to Rio each week. The metropolitan areas of Bombay and Calcutta may reach 30 million by 1985. Lagos teems with dropouts from village schools. In all of them, unemployment goes up, living standards slip. It is the ghetto city writ large across the face of the earth.

3) *The disproportion between modern technology and the labor supply:* The urban millions must be given work. This was no problem in the first growth of Atlantic cities because early industry created mass jobs for untrained workers; later, the growing sophistication of machines was matched by the growing education of a relatively stable working class. But today the developing countries confront a technology that is already immensely sophisticated and expensive and which no longer creates massive amounts of unskilled

jobs. A refinery can cost $12 million and employ only 350 people. Industry demands capital which developing nations lack and dispenses with labor of which they have too much. It also requires a steadily growing market which they cannot find at home. There the urban masses lack income, and since agriculture is stagnant, farmers cannot buy goods, and it does not take long to satisfy the small urban middle class market. Nor can would-be manufactures find sufficient openings abroad since, as we have seen, the Atlantic powers systematically increase their tariff barriers as materials are worked up to become exports of semi-manufactures and manufactured goods. If, in spite of these barriers, foreign manufactures still threaten to come in, then developed nations tend, as with textiles, to slap on a ban or a quota.

4) *The gap between savings and consumption:* Caught between population and city growth on the one hand and high-cost technology and unmodernized agriculture on the other, the developing peoples find the whole task of saving infinitely more onerous than it ever was in the Atlantic world. True, the process could be savage anywhere. But the problem of saving today is far more daunting than it ever was in Victorian times. Few workers in the early cities lived on into old age; appalling sanitation accidents kept mortality high. Children both worked and died earlier. With fewer old survivors and younger workers, non-producing consumers increased more slowly than the effective working force. Today, people do survive. They have to eat a

little. Their rising consumption takes 3 per cent off the 4.8 per cent rate of growth, slows capital formation, and makes it cruelly hard to find the savings either to transform agriculture, expand industry, or introduce essential education. The paradox is reached in which developing lands can cope with rising population and growing cities only if they have capital for modernization but cannot secure such capital because the people and the cities consume the margins available for investment.

5) *The disproportion between needs and opportunities in international trade:* * Throughout the nineteenth and early twentieth centuries one of the chief engines of growth in world trade, and hence a vital source of earnings in the developing countries, lay in the Atlantic nations' growing demand for raw materials. But a lot of evidence suggests that in the second half of the twentieth century this market mechanism is not providing the old stimulus. On the side of demand, Atlantic populations are growing much more slowly and are protecting their own farmers more systematically. Their food purchases do not expand in the old way. Where Atlantic products are competitive—beet sugar against sugar cane, the soya bean against groundnuts—the domestic farmer gets the protection. Much more efficient research and technology allows more use to be made of traditional materials and invents such substitutes as artificial rubber, plastics, and all the ar-

* A rather fuller summary of the problem can be found in Appendix C.

tificial fibres. These compete with the old sources of supply and make primary prices more unstable.

On the side of supply, the developing countries must not only compete against the Atlantic substitutes. They increasingly compete with each other—Africa piling its cocoa and coffee on top of Latin America's and entering the Indian and Ceylonese tea market. These fundamental changes have reinforced the instability and uncertainty of primary prices. A country like Colombia can see export earnings from coffee fall by a half in a single year. Ghana's cocoa prices have varied by as much as 15 per cent each year since 1959. The cost of exports from developed countries has, on the contrary, moved steadily upwards—although there have undoubtedly been offsetting gains in the quality of the goods. It is these hidden benefits that make it difficult to set down precise quantitative estimates of the profit and loss account of international trade. But a good case can be made for the judgement that in the twentieth century the old automatic mechanisms no longer stimulate an adequate worldwide momentum of development and growth.

It is this relatively discouraging background in primary output that explains the eagerness in developing countries to make more of their manufactured exports. But here again, the contradictions are formidable. Competitive manufactures tend to need large markets. Local demand is still low, because of local poverty. But mass markets in the developed world are protected against exports from the developing lands. Not only are existing products like textiles limited by quota, but products which could easily be added in the future—made-up clothing, for instance—also receive very high levels of protection. A tiny country like Hong Kong, by incredible feats of concentration and organization, can penetrate the barriers. But in general, the obstructions are greater than the opportunities.

To these we should add another semi-colonial inheritance—the control by Atlantic firms of nearly all the services involved in international trade. Banking, shipping, insurance, marketing—the profits from these essential enterprises flow back almost exclusively to the wealthy lands. Add the extent of foreign private investment which draws back profits, capital gains, and amortization, add the debts incurred on public account over the last fifteen years, and it is not surprising to learn that today, although developing nations' exports have been increasing since 1960 by 6 per cent a year, the ability to buy more imports is only just over half as great. The balance is creamed off to meet the Atlantic world's invisible earnings—insurance, shipping—and to repay debt. By 1970 such repayments are expected to absorb at least one third of all the developing world's earnings in foreign exchange.

It could, of course, be argued that the developing nations should do more to break away from traditional "North-South" patterns of trade where all the disadvantages seem to pile up against them and to explore more actively the chances of increasing their trade with each other. Clearly, this is a vital priority. Regional common markets, the regional development banks for Asia, Latin America, and Africa have this purpose high on their agendas. But it is not a quick answer. The developing nations cannot in a couple of decades supercede all the existing structures—markets, shipping lines, import-export businesses—and set up a completely new network. They cannot immediately overcome the fact that their primary exports compete with each other. They cannot avoid the fact that most of them are entering the same phase of industrialization and tend, still, to produce the same kind of goods. These are obstacles which take time and investment and sustained strategy to overcome.

And this is perhaps another way of repeating the point that, given the number of interlocking obstructions which lie in the way of modernizing the South of the planet, easy automatic solutions cannot be expected. However effective "business as usual" and reliance on nothing but the mechanisms of the world market may have been in the nineteenth century, they are unlikely to be the whole answer today. And this should not surprise us since, inside our domestic economies, we correct the market as a matter of course. All the reforms—of progressive taxation, of fairer shares through collective bargaining, of government interventions to secure high demand and stable growth—which have revolutionized Western economies in the twentieth century have all precisely been measures to offset the instabilities and obstructions inherent in the completely free workings of the market. But in the world at large, we seem to be ready to rely on the market alone.

Chapter Five

Record of Development

I N THEORY at least there
is no reason why the modifications of the market system which have helped to enrich and stabilize the developed societies should not be introduced at the level of the world economy. Three critical changes were outlined in Chapter Two—taxation to redistribute wealth and increase the skills and health of the poorer groups; a better distribution of rewards through the mechanisms of the market itself—higher wages, fringe benefits, holidays with pay; and the government's commitment to the full use of the country's resources by ensuring a sufficient pressure of demand. Of these, two have, in fact, already been considered, even rather tim-

(67)

idly practised, at the world level.

Programs of economic assistance, provided they are made up of grants or of loans on concessionary terms,* can be counted a kind of world tax or obligation. As we have seen, they transfer about $6,000 million each year from rich to poor and take perhaps 0.6 per cent of the wealthy nations' rising national income. At various times—notably at the first meeting of the United Nations Conference on Trade and Development (UNCTAD) at Geneva in 1964—the wealthy nations have suggested that they might guarantee a transfer of 1 per cent of national income. But this figure would include all kinds of profitable investment, even commercial credits for short periods at high rates of interest. It can hardly be called a genuine unrequited transfer of resources and in any case would do little for the poorest nations who make up at least half the population of the developing world and receive less than 15 per cent of all foreign private investments. If the wealthy nations decide to specify a guaranteed flow of resources—including both aid and profitable investment—then a 2 per cent minimum would be a more reasonable aim.

There are other possible ways of securing the needed flow of resources. Pope Paul VI has suggested

* Here one can cite the terms of the funds loaned for projects of high developmental priority by the International Development Association, a subsidiary of the World Bank. These loans are made only to countries with a per capita income of less than $250 and are repayable in fifty years. Repayments do not begin for ten years and the only "interest" is a service charge of three quarters of one per cent.

that the nations might abate their arms spending by a certain percentage—say, 10 per cent—and transfer the saving to a World Fund for Development. Since world arms cost each year not much less than $150,000 million, the potential saving would nearly equal the proposed 1 per cent. Or again, the citizen might find consumption taxes less onerous than a direct tax. The United States, Canada, Britain, and France spend some $50,000 million each year on alcohol and tobacco. Ten cents extra on each dollar spent would equal five sixths of the entire aid program of the Atlantic nations today. And in all this, it must be remembered that no scale of transfer proposed so far in any way *reduces* Atlantic wealth, which goes on growing by its inexorable $60,000 million a year. All that the proposals do is to suggest a very slight slowing down of the rate of further annual enrichment.

When we turn from taxation to rewards through the market, it is perhaps legitimate to compare the worldwide commercial exchanges between the rich and poor nations with the internal sharing out of purchasing power, in the nineteenth century, between owners and workers. Both are based upon a very high concentration of effective power and ownership in one small segment of the market. Both demonstrate the tendency of the market, unmodified by social or moral policies and inhibitions, to compensate the rich sector in a way that is out of all proportion to the rewards flowing to anyone else—as the Bible puts it: "to him who hath shall be given." The difference is that social reform, workers' pressure, and managerial enlightenment have vastly widened the distribution of rewards inside the domestic market. But these changes are still absent in the world at large. What could they be?

Once again, there is no shortage of possibilities. The second UNCTAD Conference in New Delhi in 1968 takes up where the last session left off, and many of the original suggestions are now being discussed with new facts and added urgency. They are all in one way or another designed to steady and increase the export incomes of the developing nations either by larger access to export markets or by enhancing the earnings these nations can make in export markets. The former methods include such policies as tariff-free entry for raw materials or preferential treatment for goods from developing countries; the latter, plans for stabilizing primary prices and for compensatory finance against shortfalls in export income.

Still other policies look to the flow of investment and the mounting burden of debt. Private enterprise operating in developing countries could arrange for more local ownership in the equity of the company. More participation in the service industries—shipping, banking—could be built up. More Western capital might be invested in research into wider possible uses for primary products—at present the bulk of the research goes to possible new processes in developed lands. Debt arrangement could be modified, for instance, by subsidies from the wealthy powers to reduce rates of interest. All such steps would increase and stabilize the

(70)

flow of resources going to poor nations through the mechanisms of the world market. Moreover, they would do so in the critical area of foreign exchange which not-yet-developed nations, by definition, cannot do without. The reason is simple. To be underdeveloped precisely means to have only the beginnings of industry and modernized agriculture. The tools and machinery of modernization must still be purchased abroad. Without adequate foreign exchange—that is to say, other peoples' currencies—this cannot be done. So the whole effort of development slows down for lack of the generators and tractors and machine tools needed to get local modernization off the ground.*

A steadier flow of export earnings, 1 per cent of national income as an "unrequited" transfer or world tax and perhaps another 1 per cent in normal investment would, of course, very greatly increase the resources available to the developing world. But such policies would not of themselves answer a deeper question. What, actually, *is* the flow of investment and earnings needed each year to accelerate and ensure the modernization of the poorer peoples? The essence of the revolution of "demand management" at home is the assessment of whether all forms of demand—for private consumption, for public spending, for public and private investment—are adequate to absorb existing resources and expand them for the future. Even if the answer is still one of considerable trial and error, which better analysis and the use of the computer is only gradually

* See Appendix C.

improving, nevertheless the question is asked. But no such enquiry is made for the world economy. No one asks: What does rapid worldwide development require? What scale of investment does it call for? To what extent does the present flow promise to do the job? If it does not, what will? It seems somewhat irrational to embark on so great an undertaking as the basic improvement of the world's housekeeping without making a rather better attempt to estimate the cost.

We know that it is a good deal higher than our present combination of dwindling aid, uncertain export earnings, and rather static investment. The World Bank has, at the moment, capital projects worth at least three quarters of the whole present flow of aid simply waiting for finance. Its bid to quadruple the funds available to IDA—from about $250 million to a billion a year—is based on a careful assessment of what could usefully be expended. Detailed studies have shown that a growth rate of 6 per cent a year could be achieved by India in the 1970s if the inflow of external resources were raised by 50 per cent. In another field, the best scientific advice in America has estimated that another $4,000 million a year should be spent on agriculture if near-starvation is to be avoided in many lands in the 1980s. And since this figure does not include essential spending on water, power, and roads, it might need to be half as high again. It is this kind of calculation, which relates expenditure to the desired objective, that the world requires if it is to add to its strategy for world growth the third and most effective element—a calculation of the needed spending, in other words, of the necessary demand.

What stands in the way? The concept has first to overcome a profound psychological obstacle—the feeling that spending a great deal of money does not give the answer and leads only to waste. This general proposition is buttressed by a whole set of special instances of supposed or reported failure. Together they create a context of thinking which is discouraged, sceptical, or downright hostile. And it is this context, rather than any particular judgement about policy, that determines peoples' reaction to any possible general strategy of world growth.

So the first thing to be said is that in a number of critical instances a very large-scale program of stimulating fresh demand—in other words, of spending—has in fact precipitated economies into unprecedented phases of growth. Indeed, the whole concept of "demand management" came out of such an experience—the experience of the sudden boost of war demand which between 1940 and 1944 doubled the scale of America's industrial economy. If anyone had proposed in 1940 to unleash $24,000 million of government-stimulated demand upon America—the 1942 defense budget—anguished cries of "economic insanity" or "bankruptcy via inflation" would have rung across the firmament. But war was the acceptable context and the American economy has not stopped growing ever since.

(73)

Similarly between 1945 and 1953, America spent over $2,000 million on postwar aid to Japan. Then between 1951 and 1953, it added some $1,300 million in defense orders as a by-product of the war in Korea. The result was to help launch an "economic miracle" which in three decades may make Japan the world's third largest industrial economy. Even South Korea, battered, fought over, ruined, is now growing busily—by better than 6 per cent a year—and one reason is that, on top of postwar aid, the struggle in Vietnam is bringing in a flood of war-sparked demand for extra supplies. Thailand, Formosa, and Turkey are other lands where rapid growth is not unconnected with massive military assistance.

Now all this is no paean of praise for war and its by-products. It is no argument for programs of military aid. When one contemplates how great a part of the world's economic growth and technological thrust are sustained and perverted by the $150,000 million spent on them each year, one must wonder whether the earth is not, after all, the lunatic asylum for the planetary system. To achieve rapid growth by piling up the instruments of destruction is, to adapt Charles Lamb's allegory, to invent roast pig by burning down the house. Smoking ruins in the Far East are a high price to pay for delicious pork in the surrounding areas.

The point, however, is not that such funds are well spent but that spending funds on that scale does, in fact, stimulate growth. In South Vietnam, under the pressures of war, two new harbours—Camranh Bay and Da Nang—have been put in, at a cost of $150 million, in less than eighteen months. There is hardly a military expert who will not point proudly to their future use in a peacetime economy. But was it necessary to have a bloody war to think on such a scale? Is imagination liberated only when destruction is at issue? Are we to be aroused by our fears and hates and never by our loves? If out of all the carnage were to come some sense of man's unlimited resources for the works of peace, then we could still reap some gain from our harvests of unreason. And one condition of such a hope is to realize that money for tractors stimulates an economy fully as much as money for tanks, that roads and bridges and ports for peace create just the same employment of men and resources as the infrastructure of destruction, that money spent building a town is no less effective than money spent destroying it, that, to sum up the whole debate, a world spending an extra $150,000 million on its own economic growth and education, on the productivity of its farms and the beauty of its cities would have an infinitely higher chance of basic security and survival than the missile-ridden, rocket-threatened, doom-laden planet we know today.

But perhaps the argument cannot be conducted simply in terms of general expenditure. Those who are sceptical of assistance are often so on the basis of some particular policy that has failed, some project that has blown up in peoples' faces, some especially flagrant, detailed example of futility and waste. That such things exist, no one denies. Assistance strategies are not in the hands of archangels. Every human program has its score of blanks and misses. But even in the compass of a few pages, it is possible to show, under every one of the five critical headings of development, examples of what has gone right and of successes that could be taken as working models for larger, stronger, and better devised strategies for the future.

Take first of all the critical emergence of a sense of national identity and of a collective will to forge a modern community. People in the Atlantic world who take their nationhood for granted and in fact need, in many ways, to mitigate it with wider loyalties, often do not realize how difficult and precarious the search for national identity is in the developing peoples' early post-colonial period. Nationalist movements which united every kind of disparate grouping—tribes and languages, mill owners and mill hands, graduates from Europe and "verandah boys"—in the struggle to be rid of colonial control, have found themselves from one day to the next compelled to invent a new kind of cement once the old rulers had hauled down the flag and departed. One cement can be the enforced dominance of one group over all the rest. Another may be an ugly frontier dispute. But of the peaceful and constructive possibilities, the kind of development plan which draws on local initiative and into which foreign assistance can be usefully inserted does offer some promise of success.

In India where 500 million people combine a hundred languages with a score of sub-cultures there is no doubt that the basic element of union is the Hindu system. But at the dynamic level of modern nation building, the national plan which, backed with foreign aid and exchange, builds the power stations, extends the roads, expands the ports, opens up the mineral reserves, and begins the distribution of fertilizer is the chief available symbol of national drive and interest. On the hydroelectric sites men toil together who have come from Trivanderum and Lucknow. In the offices of new industries, the educated Madrassi and the Punjabi work side by side. Delhi's chief instrument of economic cohesion is its control over development funds and scarce foreign exchange. No one overlooks the risks of bureaucratic centralization. But the web of the Plan and its investments remains the chief secular link of this vast community.

When we turn to literacy and the training of modern minds, we find the greatest needs and also some of the most remarkable results in Africa. In many ways, the colonial record on the field of education was not brilliant. But in the last two decades, a new energy has appeared. In the late 1940s, the British Government began the policy of setting up and helping to endow local universities in Africa—in Accra, in Ibadan, later in Kampala, Nairobi, and Dar es Salaam. Within ten years of its foundation, the University of Nigeria at Ibadan was securing as high a percentage of honours, on a per capita basis, as its parent university, London. In all these universities, lecturers and professors from the developed countries still make up a critical segment of the teaching force.

Nor is this assistance confined to university levels. The French send 29,000 teachers to Africa, nearly 23,000 of them working in primary and secondary schools. Britain provides over 3,500 trained people in teaching. Six thousand of America's Peace Corps volunteers are teachers and form an indispensable element in Africa's multiplying schools. Germany is taking a special interest in technical training. The result of all this, combined with local expenditures, which in some African states reach 50 per cent of the budget, is beginning to give the continent its first dynamic program for educated leadership and middle level cadres—without which development is impossible.

The general record of the developing nations in the accumulation of savings leaves no doubt about the new momentum of the last fifteen years. That growth is above the nineteenth century average is due above all to the fact that the average level of saving has been pushed up to between 12 and 15 per cent of gross national product and in a number of cases the marginal rate of saving—in other words, the proportion of newly created income that is saved—is nearly 30 per cent. Against this background, it should not seem surprising that, of the $46,000 million invested in developing lands today, at least 80 per cent—or over $34,000 million—has been provided by the developing peoples themselves. But they could not have achieved this level without the critical input of outside capital—in aid and private investment—for this was their provision of essential foreign exchange. When, however, one remembers that India has pushed its saving rate above 12 per cent of G.N.P. in an economy where the average per capita income is not above 70 dollars, one realizes that this is genuine saving, genuine doing without. As such, it bears little resemblance to the savings generated by wealthy communities which literally cannot consume all the vast wealth their technology spins off and save virtually from surfeit, not sacrifice.

When we turn to agriculture, we encounter some of the sharpest criticism and suspicions of the aid effort. Developing peoples, so runs the argument, have been seduced by the myth of "smoking factory chimneys," and capital assistance from abroad has condoned this childishness. Industry has had a total priority. Meanwhile, unnoticed and unopposed, the gaunt figure of hunger has stalked over the neglected fields and threatens an all but irreversible crisis of mass malnutrition and near-famine as populations bound up and food supplies stagnate. Neither through creative agricultural policies nor through a proper insistence on birth control has the strategy of foreign assistance mitigated this desperate risk. Now it may be too late.

This is too gloomy a picture. It is true that the first emphasis in many plans was on industry. This is because colonial governments did so little to foster it that it became, inevitably, a symbol of virile independence. Nor could foreign advice, however well backed with capital, impinge too effectively on this attitude in the first decade of independence. It would have suggested a conspiracy to hold back industries which might "compete" with developed interests. Nor, incidentally, could white foreigners press too hard for birth control, whatever its "cost-benefit ratio," when the suspicion could have been widespread that fewer coloured babies, not rising coloured living standards, were uppermost in the advisers' minds.

But today the situation is changing fast—for three reasons. The first is the wide open and glaring fact of lagging agriculture, the second the equal obviousness of population pressure. All round the world, governments are adopting policies of family planning and are asking for the help they might have looked at with suspicion only a decade ago. Equally they are beginning to realize that family planning and economic progress are two sides of the same coin. A man does not opt for fewer children if they are the only support of his old age or if infantile mortality is high. Moreover, lengthening life will enlarge populations for twenty years yet. The key to a more stable population lies beyond any particular kind or strategy of birth control. It lies in the general increase in economic and social confidence and elbowroom. For this reason, the third reason for a changing outlook may well be the most important—that a number of agricultural policies can be seen to work and promise to expedite with a new dynamism the whole process of development.

Take the case of Pakistan. At the beginning of the sixties, the growth of output in farming was still hardly keeping pace with a population growth of nearly 3 per cent. Then a number of decisive changes in policy were made. The farmer received more for his grain. Fertilizers and wells were subsidized heavily, credit institutions received support in the countryside, all export taxes were removed from agricultural exports. The result was a strong turning of the terms of trade in favour of the village. In other words, the farmer began to need to sell less of his own product in order to secure his supplies from the towns. As a result, the growth rate in agriculture doubled in a year or two and began to move well ahead of population. But notice that the change could hardly have been made without large-scale economic assistance running at twice the level of India's. Foreign exchange was available for imports of fertilizers and machines to manufacture wells. Surplus grain under Public Law 480 prevented rising grain prices in the towns from getting completely out of control. The whole agricultural strategy was a combined operation of internal and external policy and resources: the result, a decisive breakthrough on the agricultural front.

Experiments such as these have underlined all over again the much earlier experience of Japan—that a dynamic countryside is a precondition of sustained industrial growth. In general, industrial expansion in the developing world has been going ahead at not much less than 7 to 10 per cent a year. The installation of factories, the hiring and training of skills, the bringing in of quite a range of private investment to help with both processes have perhaps proved easier than people expected. But once the installations are done and the critical problems of marketing begin, the rural people —who make up 60 to 70 per cent of the population—need money in their pockets if sales are to prosper, if the urban migrants are to be drawn into industrial work, and if the economy is to avoid the dismal nemesis of industries without markets—which is the *unsmoking* factory chimney. In countries such as Kenya, where massive assistance to land settlement and development has enduced lively agricultural growth, the industries introduced by European settlement continue to expand and the whole economy grows by more than 7 per cent a year. In Ghana where earlier policies neglected the countryside, over-ambitious industries still run below capacity for lack of a market. But the balance can be kept and in many developing lands, industry and farming now promise to be the dual wings or engines of their economy's rising flight.

What does all this amount to? Certainly not to any claim that the modernization of the developing world is proceeding in due and peaceful fashion. The vast upheavals of modernity do not usually occur in such good order. After four decades or so of modernization, Britain saw the barns and farms alight and the machines smashed by the Luddites in the 1820s. In the United States, after a comparable spell of economic change, nine out of the twenty-five state governments were in default on their obligations—largely to Britain—and in the 1840s British bankers talked about "hayseed Americans" the way Americans now talk about unreliable Asians. We have been here before. Only, in the Atlantic world, our memories are short and our region which produced, in this century, the most violent "tribal" upheavals—between Teuton and Gaul and Anglo-Saxon and Slav—and the most devastating economic depressions now argues that difficulty and unrest in developing countries, after a couple of decades of experiment, prove their unfitness to succeed.

We forget the evidence of a common human experience. In the words of the poet, A. E. Housman:

> *There, like the wind through woods in riot,*
> *   Through him the gale of life blew high;*
> *The tree of man was never quiet:*
> *   Then 'twas the Roman, now 'tis I.*

Then it was the Atlantic nations "in riot." Now, with all the deeper and more daunting difficulties of the twentieth century, it is the rest of the human race. We cannot expect tranquility while the developing nations pour, as we have done, over the rapids of modernization. Those who look for a quiet planet had better take ship for the moon.

What the events since 1945 prove is that in spite of the upheavals, progress *is* being made, that growth *is* gathering momentum, that the problems of development are better understood, and that although between 80 and 90 per cent of the effort of modernization will be borne by the modernizing peoples themselves, the Atlantic Powers who make up the vanguard of development, whose affluence and elbowroom are already a fact, *can* play a critical part in easing and accelerating the passage to modernity. This part is the provision of the essential input of foreign exchange over and above the "normal" levels of private investment and international trade, neither of which reaches adequately the poorest nations or gives them sufficient boost to overcome the built-in contradictions of development in the last part of the twentieth century. Growth rates above the average—which *have* been achieved—would have been inconceivable without access to foreign machines, foreign skills, foreign services of all kinds. This has been the essential role of economic assistance. Cut it back and the poorer nations will be forced either into a stagnation where food and population cancel each other out or into the violent and not necessarily more successful "bootstrap" operations to which China turned when all Soviet aid was suddenly withdrawn. Neither alternative promises a better outcome. On the contrary, both point to an ever more disorderly and delinquent world.

Chapter Six

The Politics
of Affluence

THIS PROSPECT, on a smaller scale, has been faced before. As each Atlantic society began its process of development and drew the mass of the people into the new technological system based upon high saving, mechanized production, and a mass labour force, there came a time when the new possibilities and aspirations created by the system stood out in increasingly bitter contrast to its flagrant imbalance, unequal rewards, and urban misery. As the nineteenth century drew to a close, aggressive trade unionism, great strikes, violence in the streets scared cautious citizens in the United States into believing that the whole social order was being torn down around them. Anarchism grew as a force in Europe and advertized its cult of violence by carefully planned and highly visible assassinations. Russia boiled up, by way of peasant revolt, into the revolution of 1905. Even in Britain, where social peace had accompanied the great economic boom of the fifties and sixties, the mood grew more uncertain as the century waned. There were trade union riots in London in 1885 during the so-called Great Depression. Then, in the early 1900s, unrest increased again and one observer, speaking in 1909, made this analysis of the scene:

If we [carry] on in the old happy-go-lucky way, the richer classes ever growing in wealth and in number, the very poor remaining plunged or plunging ever deeper into helplessness, hopeless misery, then I think there is nothing before us but savage strife between class and class and its increasing disorganization with the increasing waste of human strength and human virtue.

The speaker was Winston Churchill, and if his forecast proved wrong, it was in part because he himself at that time was deeply engaged in a most strenuous effort to introduce social insurance, end sweated labour, extend labour exchanges, impose minimum wage standards, and achieve a system of pensions for the aged. Where no such efforts were made—in Czarist Russia, for instance, or later in the miserable inter-war wreckage of China's 1911 Republic—the prediction proved correct. Once the mass of the people reach a certain level of awareness—of opportunity, of frustration—there are only two ways forward for society: to reform or blow up. There is every reason to suppose that in a planetary society in many ways more open, accessible, and aware of itself than was Russia or the United States in the 1880s, the choices are the same.

To those who believe that such a society can survive, to borrow the phrase of Mr. George Woods, former President of the World Bank, "half sated and half starved," that it can be held down by force or persuaded to forget the vast and growing disproportions between rich and poor, that the old "happy-go-lucky way" of keeping 80 per cent of the resources for 20 per cent of the people will peacefully endure, one can only say that every evidence of history refutes their optimism. Two thirds of humanity are on the verge of realizing what is the true context of wealth and poverty, affluence and misery, opportunity and frustration in this narrow world. Without reforms, without new ventures of generosity and justice, without sustained efforts of social innovation, then Winston Churchill's verdict, reversed at home precisely by such policies, could still be tragically vindicated in the world at large.

This is not an exercise designed to try, like Charles Dickens's Fat Boy, "to make yer flesh creep." It is a sober analysis of the only historical analogies we possess to guide us in policy-making today. And the chief reason why its relevance may seem dubious brings us back, once again, to the problem of context. We simply do not think about our planet as a community. We do not accept the comparison between what Professor Toynbee has called the "internal proletariat" and the "external proletariat," between the poor at home and the poor abroad. The nationalist framework of all our training keeps the poverty of the world at large outside our vision, beyond the reach of our imagination, and far away from any commitment of justice and good will. We live in the strangest dispensation in which lines on a map hem in the flow of wealth, pile it up higher and higher in one corner of the globe, and allow little of the spill-over that ended the exclusiveness of the feudal or Victorian elite and created the modern mass economy. Yet over, above, through, and round those same lines, the world surges on—in flight, in vision, in electronics, in trade, in wealth and ruin. Everything is unified, except our instruments of policy and our will to act. This is the basic reason for the paradoxes of our time. Our needs, our web of work and wealth, our institutions based upon gain—or upon fear—are worldwide in their impact. But the means of expressing our moral and humane obligations, our sense of justice and solidarity, our concern and our neighbourly love—these means are so weak that they can barely lift themselves over the lines on the map.

This is not an economic issue. It is political and moral. Societies growing in wealth by some $60,000 million a year are not confronted by any severe physical limitations on their ability to extend aid or share their increasing wealth more widely. No one doubts, for instance, that should the United States decide to spend anything from $5 billion to $50 billion on a new anti-missile system, the resources will be forthcoming. Particular difficulties such as the alleged strain of foreign aid on the balance of payments can be eased by "tying" aid—in other words, by seeing to it that all dollars are spent in America, all sterling in Britain. In any case, if the whole ring of wealthy states were all equally determined to aid development, they would make mutual arrangements to see that extra aid did *not* increase the strain—for instance, by agreeing not to convert into gold the proportion of currency represented by further capital assistance.

Similarly, if political leaders plead the impossibility of increasing internal budgetary commitments to economic assistance, they simply mean a *political* impossibility. Voters want the next annual round of growth in the economy—not less than $40,000 million in the case of the United States—to be spent on something else. Economically, $4,000 million more for aid would hardly be noticed. But political priorities are something else again and the next 3 or 4 per cent increase in national resources will follow them—for more defence, rebuilding the cities, coloured television, mink ear muffs, or whatever else the community believes to be of higher priority than pulling the rest of the human race across the threshold of the abundant life.

But in confronting what are basically political and

moral decisions, we have the formidable hurdle of national exclusiveness to cross. The task is not, in the first place, to convince the citizens in wealthy countries that poverty should be attacked, opportunities increased, and a larger measure of justice extended to all the people. On balance, this battle, whose outcome seemed grim and uncertain only fifty years ago, has been largely won in Europe; and in the United States, it is hard to believe that the chief exception—urban poverty in the ghettoes—will be left to fester. The battle today is to convince the citizens who accept responsibility at home to accept it equally across the frontiers, across the lines on the map. And this is much more formidable.

We are all born tribalists. We all still live in the pre-technological structure of limited, separate, territorially circumscribed communities. We still derive our emotions from the millennia during which resources were scarce and the tribe or the empire or the nation were devices to safeguard a static share, if necessary by raiding and seizing other peoples' wealth. Even though wealth these days depends less and less on particular countries and more and more on the shared universe of men's minds, ideas, and research, we are hard put to it to overcome the emotional and territorial instincts bred of thousands of years of aggressive-protective conflict. Beneath our well washed skins and sophisticated hairdos still lurks the savage face of fearful, hungry, marauding tribal man. And the fact that nationalism was the first forcing house of the new technological society only increases our sense of its necessity. Like day-old chicks, we still find the world strange outside the incubator.

But to say that the task of persuasion and conversion is difficult does not mean that it should not be attempted or cannot be done. In the 1850s, Disraeli wrote of Britain as "two nations—the nation of the rich and the nation of the poor." The gulf between them was so great that he could describe it only in terms of the vast barriers which nationhood sets up between peoples of different culture and background. He did not, at that time, believe that the gulf could easily be bridged. His fear, indeed, was that it could not. But in the event, he underestimated the amount of reason, enlightened self-interest, informed apprehension and moral compassion the reformers could call on. Possibly we make the same underestimate today.

If we begin with the crudest motive—fear of violence and revolt—it is true that the sense of the Cold War has abated. The split between Russia and China has made obsolete all manner of dire foreboding about the "Sino-Soviet bloc" and its uncompromising hostility. Mechanized hordes of Communist divisions no longer threaten to sweep through Europe or Asia. However wasteful and terrifying, the nuclear deterrent at the level of the super-powers seems to work. On the other hand, the war in Vietnam has shown with what savage effectiveness guerrilla armies can take on forces that are vastly superior to them in equipment and firepower. If the big wars are contained, the small wars may not be, and the ordinary methods and weapons of modern war do not seem too effective in containing them. Possibly, then, they could be fought more effectively with less lethal instruments—with land reform, with cooperatives, with fertilizer and market roads, with urban housing, with the hope of schools and jobs. Land settlement has turned the dark lands of the Mau Mau into a lively, growing Kikuyu farming area. Rural works and cooperatives have brought some stability to some of the world's most overcrowded farm lands in East Pakistan. Earlier land reforms seem to lessen the appeal of guerrillas to the Bolivian peasant just as, first in the 1870s and then again under General MacArthur, they have stabilized and enriched the Japanese countryside.

Some people, of course, argue that neither armies nor aid need be considered. Let the poor go their own way while the Atlantic states, in isolated affluence, leave them to it. But it is difficult to envisage an American totally indifferent to a score of Cubas in Latin America. It is difficult to conceive of Europe steering completely clear of a long, desperate race war in Southern Africa. In the Middle East, the stakes are high enough to recreate the "Balkan" spiral, outside nations being drawn in to war by the struggles of local client states. In all these situations, sustained aid is not certain to contain or prevent conflict. But at least it has a chance of lessening the pressures that lead up to conflict. Of few other policies can so much be said.

Enlightened self interest points in the same direction. It is true that the developing world accounts for only about 20 per cent of the world's wealth and trade. Its trade with the wealthy nations is lower still—it provides only 14 per cent of their imports. Given their built-in capacities to raise output and increase productivity, they can in theory get on comfortably without the rest of the world. Yet they are intensely competitive. Their industrial goods jostle each other in the same markets. The response of many industries in the United States to livelier competition through falling tariffs is to demand the protection of a quota system. American food farmers resent Europe's protective agricultural levies. And the Atlantic stomach cannot push consumption beyond a certain point. All this suggests that, for Atlantic traders, a penumbra of over 2 billion people increasing their demands and their consumption and production enough to pay for the goods they want would be an admirable reassurance against the tougher forms of inter-Atlantic competition. Investment in development does raise skills and enlarge markets. As such, it is a useful if not an absolutely indispensable program against the day when "normal commerce" will have put colour TV in every room from Vladivostok to New York, and industry asks: Where next?

Even if we are not moved by either fear or profit, there are other motives—of reason, of good will, of conscience—and these played as large a part in domestic reform as any fear of the mob or hope of business interest. One needs no more than a reasonable acquaintance with history to realize that civil order is best maintained in societies with functioning institutions of law and police to see that peace is kept, and functioning policies of justice and welfare to see that it is worth keeping. This recognition of *fact* lies behind mankind's first experiments, in this century, with international peacekeeping through the United Nations and with international welfare and development through the World Bank, the U.N. Development Program, and all the other functional international agencies. If the world were not seen to be so small, vulnerable, and interdependent, these experiments would not have been undertaken. If the world were less "tribal," less divided and hostile, they would have been pursued more vigorously. But there at least they stand, a tribute to man's groping attempts to oppose reason to the drives of his millennial instincts. For it really does not stretch rationality very far to believe that nations cannot take themselves out of a world society which the astronaut strides round in 90 minutes—and science can blow up in 90 seconds. And if the nations are "in" without escape hatches, then clearly it is better to build and support the worldwide institutions—of peacekeeping, of development, of welfare—which in any society maintain the peace and in a nuclear society can prevent annihilation.

The trouble, it must be repeated, is that most traditional and customary feelings tend to point the other way: to withdrawal, to isolation, to obsessive concern with local interests, to indifference to the larger world.

So reason, today, requires reinforcement from deeper commitments, from emotions which have some of the rootedness of tribal or nationalist devotion but not its large irrelevance to present reality. At this point, we return to where we started—to the vision society carries of its meaning and purpose, to the force of the images with which it tries to "invent" its future, to the picture not of where it is but of where it would like to be. And this, for the modern world, is still bound up with the vision of the unity of man.

We cannot escape it. The sense of a common, shared humanity—which is what we mean by the equality and unity of the human experiment—explodes in every revolution of the modern world. From the vision of the American Revolution, in which equal men came together for the political task of government, flows the Wilsonian concept of an orderly international system in which nations, equal in self-determination, come together to build a peaceful world. It is, in a sense, a highly respectable, gentlemanly version of humanity's travail. Yet it accepts the revolutionary need to pass beyond the nation in order to organize the world. From France and Marx and Russia, we inherit the turbulent, passionate version of the same faith. Now it is a question not of political forms and constitutional guarantees but of economic and social substance. Mankind will find out its unity when the barriers of exploitation and inequality have been thrown down; and the human family, in a world from which all states have withered away, will live in the perfect fraternity of shared and equal wealth.

Each version leaves out what the other brings in. The Americans have not shown much sense of the tragic incidence of inequality, exploitation, violence, and misery in the world on top of which an orderly international system is to be built up. The Russians have shown a remarkable lack of understanding of the political instruments, rule of law, and tough sacrifices of sovereignty demanded by a system in which Communist states, far from withering away, grow stronger and engage in all the traditional brouhaha of high diplomacy—frontier disputes, troop movements, spies, removals of envoys and long-range shouting matches. But the point here is not the deficiencies and imbalances of the two versions but rather the degree to which they are both committed, in their view of the world, to the single, inescapable community of man.

And this is not, after all, surprising, since both have their roots in the vision of humanity first formulated in the great ethical revolution of the world religions and transmitted to Western society through the mediation of Judeo-Christian culture. No doubt Chinese Communists will accept only with enormous reserve the idea of Western influences on Mao's thoughts. Russian Marxists tend to look no further than Lenin and Marx for their inheritance. But the situation in the Western world is odder still. Again and again, we hear its claim to be a "Christian civilization." But if it is, what do Christians suppose the words really mean? *Can* they mean that at a time when wealth beyond human imagining has been unlocked among the Atlantic nations by science and technology, their "Christian" response is to roll up the national income at a rate of $60,000 million a year and let the rest of the world fester in its miseries? This is a curious outcome for a faith in which Dives and Lazarus have become the symbols of selfish wealth heading for disaster and of helpless poverty waiting to be raised up.

Christians, of course, will disclaim selfishness, and indeed one can argue that it is not *intended* selfishness. The trouble, as we have seen, is that their indifference is rooted in something supposedly much more respectable—the total claims of national sovereignty and the explicit lack of obligations that go beyond national frontiers. We need no further explanation to tell us why national societies which will spend what is needed to build up a backward, poverty-stricken *Mezzogiorno* in Southern Italy or restore pockets of poverty like Appalachia have no sustained or unquestioned commitment to counter the infinitely deeper poverty of Andean villagers or the street-sleepers of Bombay. National governments have obligations only to national citizens. In return, citizens take these limits for granted, and so, at the frontiers, the flow of wealth, the sense of duty, the sustained and creative effort threatens to come to a full stop.

But can Christians accept such limits? Are they no more than nationalists or tribalists? Is their faith based on the formula "I will love my neighbour as myself—provided he is a fellow-American, Briton, Frenchman, German"? Must we rewrite every parable in the Bible to point out that the man in the ditch was really a Samaritan too, that Christ explicitly established that all the lepers were Jews before He cleansed them, that His condition for a cure was that the dumb man would only speak Hebrew, that the Centurion himself and his servant, far from being praised as Gentiles, had to accept citizenship in Israel before the healing words could be spoken?

If Christians allow their conscience to become thus determined by nation and race and culture, they can make no response to the profound and mysterious image of the Son of Man. They will not recognise "the least of these little ones" if the face is brown or black or yellow. They will staunch the flowing charity of God Himself and dam it up behind the arbitrary frontiers imposed by men across the wide bounty of the universe. And if this is their response to the deepest mystery of their faith—God's fatherhood of all mankind, God's providence which falls on just and unjust alike, God's love which embraces the whole family of man—then they will no doubt call down on the civilization they miscall Christian the anathema of destruction which Christ Himself defined for those who do not seek and find Him in every child of man. This is the full meaning and measure of the crisis which the Christian world confronts, a crisis forged in its complacency, confirmed in its indifference, and sealed by the judgement of a God who is not mocked.

To reverse the trend may seem an almost overwhelming task. But it has been done before, and we should take courage. Some two hundred years ago, the outlook was fully as daunting for a small group of devoted men and women who set out in England to abolish the greatest evil of their day—the trans-Atlantic traffic in slaves which was growing, decade by decade, as the large-scale cultivation of sugar and then cotton in the Americas sucked in more and more manpower from a demoralized Africa. The Abolitionists faced some of the largest vested interests and most entrenched commercial ventures of their day. Influential cities like Bristol and Liverpool believed that not only their prosperity but their survival depended upon the slave trade. So did their merchants and mariners and shipwrights. Indeed, a good case could be made for the argument that Britain's whole ability to operate its vast seaborne network of commerce between the Caribbean, North America, Europe, and the East Indies turned upon its access to gold and slaves along the tragic coasts of the Benin Bight. This was the formidable battery of national self interest and economic advantage the Abolitionists set themselves to overcome.

Their methods could be a model to any groups—Christian, liberal, humane, radical—who believe today that grinding but remediable poverty is the contemporary form of slavery endured by a large part of the human race. They drew upon Christian reserves of conviction and dedication. Quakers, Methodists, Evangelicals were in the van. But they cooperated with all men of whatever persuasion—or no persuasion—who were ready to pursue the same ends. They organized meetings. They published fact sheets and pamphlets. They harassed members of parliament and created a strong parliamentary lobby with the totally disinterested and heartily revered William Wilberforce as its leader. They took advantage of the new, more liberal theories of commerce with which Adam Smith scattered the Mercantilists and argued that the country could prosper without the horrors of the Middle Passage. Working in season and out of season, without any slackening of their pressure on people and leaders alike, they at last convinced their country that the price of slavery was too high for any Christian community to tolerate and secured—in 1811—an end to the traffic and, some two decades later, the freeing of all the slaves.

Today, parliamentary systems throughout the Atlantic world are far more open to the electors' pressure. A determined minority may become the swing factor in the electorate which determines how the elections will be won. So those running for office take care, if possible, to offend no effective group with decided and well organized views. If citizens in each of the affluent countries were prepared to organize themselves in a pressure group to secure, say, the transfer of 1 per cent of national income in genuine aid to world development and give their campaign the kind of energy and staying power the Abolitionists kept up in their day, the basic financing of foreign assistance would undoubtedly be secured before the seventies had reached the halfway mark. But so long as the lobbies of the so-called Christian countries are concerned wholly with interests and only marginally with ideas and visions, there seems all too little chance that any "Abolitionist" campaign will be brought up to date with a total commitment to fight the world's present slaveries of ignorance and sickness and hunger, with a lasting dedication to the wants of millions caught in a new "middle passage" between want and opportunity, between despair and hope.

Yet to be content with anything less is to miss the whole scale of the moral challenge of our day—which is nothing less than the ability of our civilization to redeem its wealth, turn its immense resources to the service of life, and use the technology of abundance to recreate, not destroy, the face of the earth.

Appendices

Appendix A

A. SUMMARY

GROSS NATIONAL PRODUCT AND POPULATION
CLASSIFIED BY VERY POOR, POOR, MIDDLE-INCOME,
AND RICH COUNTRIES

| | GNP | | Population Projections | | |
Group	Millions of dollars	Dollars per capita	1966 (millions)	Growth rate, % increase	Increase 1965–66 (thousands)
Very Poor Countries					
(Less than $100 per capita)	139,510	69	1,691.8	1.9	36,468
Poor Countries					
($100–$249 per capita)	77,642	181	462.5	3.8	13,126
Middle-Income Countries					
($250–$749 per capita)	104,127	427	241.4	1.9	5,379
Rich Countries					
($750 per capita and up)	1,504,096	1,467	942.8	1.2	11,214
GRAND TOTAL	1,825,375	536	3,338.5	2.2	66,197

(105)

B. DETAILS

Gross National Product and Population Classified by Very Poor, Poor, Middle-Income, and Rich Countries

VERY POOR COUNTRIES (Less than $100 per capita)

Country	Year	GNP Per capita U.S. dollars	GNP Total million U.S. dollars	Population 1966 (millions)	Population Growth rate, % increase	Population Increase 1965–66 (thousands)
Afghanistan	1965	66	1,034	16.2	2.1	350
Bechuanaland	1960–62	65	22	0.4	1.1	5
Burma	1965	64	1,586	25.3	2.2	560
Burundi	1965	47	151	2.9	2.2	60
Central African Rep.	1965	77	104	1.3	1.1	15
Chad	1965	66	218	3.0	1.6	50
China (Mainland)	1965	86	60,537	716.2	1.8	12,700
Congo (Brazzaville)	1963	40	40	0.9	1.4	15
Congo (Dem. Rep. of)	1965	65	1,010	15.6	1.8	300
Dahomey	1965	62	147	2.1	2.0	40
Ethiopia	1965	54	1,214	21.0	1.8	300
Gabon	1965	53	117	0.5	0.6	5
Guinea, Rep. of	1965	73	257	3.5	2.3	80
Haiti	1965	70	306	4.8	2.5	125
India	1965	88	43,000	494.6	2.5	12,365
Indonesia	1965	85	8,884	107.9	2.3	2,500
Kenya	1965	85	800	9.4	2.3	215
Laos	1965	64	169	2.0	2.3	45
Malagasy Rep.	1965	79	508	6.3	2.7	170
Malawi	1965	40	156	4.2	0.3	15
Mali	1965	61	279	4.5	2.1	95
Nepal	1965	66	667	10.3	2.1	215
Niger	1965	71	236	3.2	2.1	65
Nigeria	1965	78	4,512	59.8	3.1	1,855
Pakistan	1965	85	9,709	116.0	2.8	3,250
Rwanda	1965	49	152	2.9	1.2	35
Somali, Rep.	1965	54	135	2.2	1.8	40
Sudan	1965	95	290	13.5	2.5	335

Country	Year	GNP Per capita U.S. dollars	GNP Total million U.S. dollars	Population 1966 (millions)	Population Growth rate, % increase	Population Increase 1965–66 (thousands)
Tanzania	1965	68	713	10.4	2.0	210
Togo	1966	93	153	1.6	2.1	35
Upper Volta	1965	52	253	4.8	1.6	80
Viet Nam (North)	1965	90	1,711	19.5	1.3	248
Yemen	1965	88	440	5.0	2.9	100
TOTAL		69	139,510	1,691.8	1.9	36,468

(cont.) GROSS NATIONAL PRODUCT AND POPULATION . . .

POOR COUNTRIES ($100–$249 per capita)

Country	Year	GNP Per capita U.S. dollars	GNP Total million U.S. dollars	Population 1966 (millions)	Population Growth rate, % increase	Population Increase 1965–66 (thousands)
Algeria	1965	211	2,500	12.9	2.8	360
Bolivia	1965	148	547	4.2	2.4	100
Brazil	1965	224	18,388	83.8	2.9	2,430
Cambodia	1965	119	728	6.6	2.8	185
Cameroon	1965	106	554	4.4	1.2	50
Ceylon	1965	140	1,569	11.8	3.1	400
China (Taiwan)	1965	203	2,520	12.5	2.5	310
Dominican Republic	1965	234	847	3.7	3.6	150
Ecuador	1965	188	970	5.2	3.0	200
El Salvador	1965	249	730	3.0	3.2	100
Ghana	1965	226	1,752	8.0	3.0	235
Honduras	1965	201	458	2.2	3.5	60
Iran	1965	226	5,594	23.1	2.4	550
Iraq	1965	223	828	8.5	3.4	300
Ivory Coast	1965	212	814	3.6	2.0	70
Jordan	1965	218	430	2.1	3.3	70
Korea (North)	1965	191	2,310	11.4	2.2	246
Korea (South)	1965	121	3,447	29.5	2.9	855

(*cont.*) GROSS NATIONAL PRODUCT AND POPULATION . . .

Country	Year	GNP Per capita U.S. dollars	GNP Total million U.S. dollars	Population 1966 (millions)	Population Growth rate, % increase	Population Increase 1965–66 (thousands)
Liberia	1965	185	198	1.0	1.1	10
Mauritania	1965	151	159	0.7	0.7	5
Morocco	1965	179	2,379	14.1	3.8	535
Oceania	1965	216	713	3.7	4.0	150
Papua and New Guinea	1965	128	276	0.7	3.0	20
Paraguay	1965	201	409	2.0	2.7	55
Philippines	1965	146	4,718	33.5	3.5	1,170
Rhodesia	1965	221	940	4.4	2.2	100
Saudi Arabia	1965	207	1,397	6.9	2.0	140
Senegal	1965	168	588	3.4	1.6	55
Sierra Leone	1965	137	324	2.8	2.1	60
Swaziland	1965	235	88	0.3	3.1	10
Syria	1965	191	1,013	5.7	3.2	180
Thailand	1965	117	3,594	32.2	3.2	1,030
Tunisia	1965	201	888	4.7	2.2	105
Turkey	1965	234	7,276	32.7	2.9	950
Uganda	1965	101	756	7.5	1.9	140
U.A.R.	1965	151	4,457	30.7	3.0	920
Viet Nam (South)	1965	108	1,748	35.2	2.3	810
Zambia	1965	198	735	3.8	0.3	10
TOTAL		181	77,642	462.5	3.8	13,126

(*cont.*) Gross National Product and Population . . .

MIDDLE-INCOME COUNTRIES ($250–$749 per capita)

Country	Year	GNP Per capita U.S. dollars	GNP Total million U.S. dollars	Population 1966 (millions)	Population Growth rate, % increase	Population Increase 1965–66 (thousands)
Barbados	1965	373	91	0.3	1.1	5
Bulgaria	1965	478	3,923	8.3	0.8	66
Chile	1965	484	4,159	8.8	2.5	220
Colombia	1965	262	4,734	18.3	2.9	530
Costa Rica	1965	380	544	1.5	3.8	60
Cuba	1965	329	2,511	7.7	2.0	150
Cyprus	1965	638	379	0.6	0.7	5
Greece	1965	597	5,104	8.9	2.9	260
Guatemala	1965	301	1,336	4.4	3.0	130
Honduras, British	1965	333	35	0.1	3.0	5
Hong Kong	1965	497	1,835	3.9	3.0	120
Jamaica	1962	464	829	1.7	1.4	25
Lebanon	1965	447	1,076	2.1	2.8	60
Libya	1965	489	791	1.4	2.2	40
Malaysia	1965	262	2,467	11.7	3.2	375
Malta	1965	451	144	0.3	0.8	5
Mauritius	1965	225	167	0.8	2.5	20
Mexico	1965	434	18,521	42.9	3.5	1,500
Nicaraqua	1965	317	525	1.7	3.5	60
Panama	1965	461	575	1.1	3.0	35
Peru	1965	305	3,549	11.9	2.8	335
Portugal	1965	367	3,379	9.2	1.5	50
Rumania	1965	436	8,296	19.5	1.0	193
South Africa	1965	523	9,636	18.4	2.8	525
Spain	1965	575	18,181	32.0	1.0	320
Surinam	1965	341	114	0.4	3.0	15
Trinidad and Tobago	1965	616	600	1.0	2.8	20
Uruguay	1965	549	1,491	2.8	1.1	30
Yugoslavia	1965	468	9,135	19.7	1.1	220
TOTAL		427	104,127	241.4	1.9	5,379

(*cont.*) GROSS NATIONAL PRODUCT AND POPULATION . . .

RICH COUNTRIES ($750 per capita up)

		GNP		Population		
Country	Year	Per capita U.S. dollars	Total million U.S. dollars	1966 (millions)	Growth rate, % increase	Increase 1965–66 (thousands)
Albania	1965	793	547	1.9	3.4	64
Argentina	1965	764	17,084	23.2	1.6	370
Australia	1965	1,754	19,925	11.5	1.7	190
Austria	1965	1,076	7,808	7.2	0.2	15
Belgium	1965	1,536	14,539	9.4	0.5	50
Canada	1965	2,100	41,171	20.2	1.9	375
Czechoslovakia	1965	905	12,810	14.2	0.8	113
Denmark	1965	1,735	8,254	4.8	0.7	30
Finland	1965	1,548	7,139	4.7	0.8	40
France	1965	1,615	78,999	48.1	0.7	300
Germany (East)	1965	1,255	21,365	17.3	0.2	159
Germany, Fed. Rep. of	1965	1,625	95,971	55.8	0.4	200
Hungary	1965	869	8,822	10.2	0.3	31
Iceland	1965	1,630	313	0.2	1.6	3
Ireland	1965	830	2,386	2.8	0.1	5
Israel	1965	1,129	2,894	2.4	2.1	50
Italy	1965	962	49,618	51.6	0.7	1,550
Japan	1965	765	74,981	98.3	0.8	800
Kuwait	1965	3,272	1,554	0.4	4.8	20
Luxembourg	1965	1,819	602	0.3	0.5	2
Netherlands	1965	1,360	16,721	12.3	1.0	210
New Zealand	1965	1,794	4,737	2.7	2.1	60
Norway	1965	1,618	6,025	3.8	0.9	35
Poland	1965	793	24,979	31.0	1.3	410
Puerto Rico	1965	987	2,598	2.6	1.6	40
Sweden	1965	2,127	16,449	7.7	0.6	45
Switzerland	1965	2,150	12,781	5.8	0.6	35
U.S.S.R.	1965	1,000	230,700	232.3	1.3	2,937
United Kingdom	1965	1,550	84,642	54.2	0.4	220
United States	1965	3,240	630,457	196.9	1.3	2,530
Venezuela	1965	828	7,225	9.0	3.6	325
TOTAL		1,467	1,504,096	942.8	1.2	11,214

SOURCE: Official Statistics

Appendix B

1) Table I gives the level of financial resources made available by governments to developing countries and international agencies between 1955 and 1965. The actual money at the disposal of the recipients is somewhat lower because amortization and interest payments have to be subtracted. For 1965, for instance, the net figure is $5,315 million.

2) Table II gives the flow of official aid as a percentage of the donors' national income. It should be noted that both Canada and the Netherlands have committed themselves to reaching the 1 per cent target. The decline in the official contribution of the United States has continued. It may not be much above 0.4 per cent in 1967.

3) The flow of development capital through international and multilateral agencies has been increasing in the 1960s. The strictly international donors—the World Bank and its affiliates and the U.N. agencies—still provide less than 20 per cent of the total flow of official aid,

TABLE I (Million U.S. Dollars)

DAC Countries	1956	1957	1958	1959	1960	1961	1962	1963	1964	1965	1966
Australia	34	42	48	50	58.9	70.9	73.8	96.9	(104)	121.6	128.8
Austria	—	−1	2	7	−0.1	2.2	13.8	2.1	14.6	33.8	36.9
Belgium	20	20	23	79	101.0	92.1	79.8	89.9	81.7	112.4	92.1
Canada	30	48	91	60	75.2	61.5	54.4	98.0	127.7	124.3	208.5
Denmark	3	2	5	13	5.5	8.1	7.4	9.7	10.6	12.9	26.1
France	647	819	884	835	848.3	943.3	977.0	850.7	831.2	752.2	721.1
Germany	142	275	268	332	351.0	618.4	467.8	437.2	423.2	471.6	490.0
Italy	43	164	73	84	110.4	85.3	110.1	110.2	54.1	92.7	117.8
Japan	96	92	285	150	97.7	108.5	88.2	140.3	115.7	243.7	285.3
Netherlands	48	23	40	49	35.3	55.9	65.0	37.8	49.2	69.2	95.3
Norway	8	9	—	5	10.1	9.0	6.9	20.6	17.1	11.8	13.4
Portugal	3	2	1	17	36.9	43.8	40.8	51.1	61.9	21.2	24.5
Sweden	3	12	4	18	6.7	8.4	18.5	22.9	32.8	38.1	56.4
United Kingdom	205	234	276	377	407.0	456.8	421.0	414.5	493.4	480.6	501.4
United States	2,006	2,091	2,410	2,322	2,776.0	3,447.0	3,536.0	3,699.0	3,445.0	3,626.8	3,634.0
TOTAL	3,288	3,832	4,411	4,398	4,919.9	6,011.2	5,960.5	6,080.5	5,860.7	6,212.7	(6,431.7)

SOURCE: Organization for Economic Cooperation and Development (OECD)

TABLE II

Total official flow, net

DAC Countries	1962	1963	1964	1965	1966
Australia	0.53	0.63	0.62	0.68	0.67
Austria	0.25	0.04	0.22	0.48	0.49
Belgium	0.77	0.81	0.66	0.84	0.64
Canada	0.19	0.32	0.39	0.35	0.52
Denmark	0.12	0.16	0.15	0.16	0.30
France	1.76	1.39	1.24	1.06	0.95
Germany	0.69	0.60	0.53	0.55	0.54
Italy	0.33	0.28	0.13	0.20	0.24
Japan	0.19	0.27	0.19	0.36	0.37
Netherlands	0.59	0.32	0.35	0.44	0.55
Norway	0.17	0.47	0.35	0.22	0.23
Portugal	1.63	1.90	2.11	0.65	0.70
Sweden	0.16	0.18	0.23	0.25	0.34
United Kingdom	0.64	0.60	0.66	0.61	0.60
United States	0.77	0.76	0.66	0.64	0.60
TOTAL	0.72	0.69	0.61	0.60	0.57

SOURCE: OECD

but their share is growing, especially if the International Development Association obtains its proposed authorization—a billion dollars a year—and the U.N. Development Program can reach its target of $200 million a year. Both these agencies are of particular importance to the poorest lands—the lands whose per capita income is below $250. The IDA does not operate anywhere else. The UNDP operates strictly on grants against which it secures matching funds, thus stimulating local self-help and generating local resources.

(113)

TABLE III (*Million U.S. Dollars*)

Agencies	1960	1961	1962	1963	1964	1965	1966
INTERNATIONAL AGENCIES							
The International Bank for Reconstruction and Development (World Bank)	516	528	507	624	574	837	603
World Bank affiliates:							
The International Development Association	—	181	187	210	425	191	457
The International Finance Corporation (for loans to private industry)	19	13	23	14	22	21	54
The U.N. Agencies *	123	200	182	229	261	260	250
MULTILATERAL AGENCIES							
The Inter-American Development Bank	—	167	121	211	205	318	396
The European Economic Community	81	147	178	72	78	277	192
TOTAL	739	1,236	1,197	1,360	1,565	1,904	1,952

* The share of the U.N. Development Program (created by the fusion in 1965/66 of the U.N. Special Fund and the Expanded Program of Technical Assistance) has risen from just under $100 million in 1961 to about $150 million in 1966.

Appendix C

1) Over the last decade and a half, the export incomes of developing peoples have risen—from $21.1 billion in 1953 to $36.6 billion in 1965.

TABLE IV

EXPORTS OF LESS DEVELOPED AREAS BY
DESTINATION, 1953 AND 1959–65
(*billions of U.S. dollars f.o.b. and percentages
of world exports*)

Year	Industrial Areas [a]		Eastern Trading Area [b]		Less Developed Areas [c]		Total World [d]	
	value	per cent	value	per cent	value	per cent	value	per cent
1953	15.1	19.3	0.3	0.4	5.2	6.7	21.1	27.0
1959	18.3	16.1	1.0	0.9	5.8	5.2	25.8	22.8
1960	19.3	15.3	1.2	1.0	6.1	4.9	27.3	21.8
1961	19.3	14.7	1.5	1.1	6.2	4.7	27.7	21.0
1962	20.3	14.6	1.6	1.2	6.4	4.6	28.9	20.9
1963	22.3	14.7	1.7	1.1	6.7	4.4	31.5	20.8
1964	24.4	14.4	1.9	1.1	7.2	4.2	34.4	20.3
1965	25.8	14.0	2.4	1.3	7.5	4.1	36.6	19.9

[a] OECD countries plus Finland and Yugoslavia. OECD countries are listed in Appendix B.

[b] The "centrally planned economies," i.e., Albania, Bulgaria, Czechoslovakia, East Germany, Hungary, Poland, Rumania, USSR, mainland China, Mongolia, North Korea, and North Vietnam.

[c] All other countries except Australia, New Zealand, and South Africa.

[d] Including Australia, New Zealand, and South Africa.

SOURCE: *GATT International Trade*, 1965

(115)

2) But this figure is misleading. It masks the fact that the *share* of the poorer nations in world trade is falling—from 27 per cent in 1953 to 19.9 in 1965. It also covers up the uncomfortable likelihood that they will have to go on producing and exporting more and more to earn the same income, let alone increase it, for the value per unit of exported goods has fallen for the primary products which they chiefly supply and risen for manufactures which they chiefly purchase.

TABLE V

UNIT VALUE OF WORLD EXPORTS (*indices 1953 = 100*)

	1953	1957	1958	1959	1960	1961	1962	1963	1964	1965
World Total	100	103	100	99	100	99	99	100	102	103
Primary products of poorer countries	100	101	96	93	93	91	90	92½	95	(94)
Manufactured imports of poorer countries	100	104	103	103	105	105½	105	105	107	109

SOURCE: As for Table I

Thus they have to sell more abroad in order to buy the same volume of imports. In other words, the "terms of trade" have turned against them. Nor is this a steady trend which they can take into account in their longer term planning. Primary producers suffer from wild variations in their prices. Changes of 15 or 20 per cent over twelve months are quite usual for primary products whereas the producers of manufactures—mainly the developed nations—have experienced a steady and sustained improvement in their terms of trade over the last decade.

The irregularities experienced by primary producers are bad enough under any conditions, but they are devastating in countries with only one or two possible lines of export.

(116)

TABLE VI

PRIMARY EXPORTING COUNTRIES: CONCENTRATION
OF EXPORTS, 1936–1938, 1953–1955, AND 1959–1961

*Percentage of total exports accounted for
by three principal commodities in:*

Country	1936–38	1953–55	1959–61	Commodities in 1959–61
Argentina	81	71	86	Meats, cereals, and wool
Australia	68	63	60	Wool, wheat, and meat
Bolivia	74	82	74	Tin ore, lead ore, and tungsten ore
Brazil	69	81	65	Coffee, cocoa, and cotton
Burma	81	82	79	Rice, teakwood, metals, and ores
Ceylon	91	90	90	Tea, rubber, and coconut products
Chile	74	80	76	Copper, nitrates, and wood
China (Taiwan)	—	80	54	Sugar, fruit, and rice
Colombia	90	97	92	Coffee, petroleum, vegetable seeds, oils, fruits, and nuts
Congo (Leopoldville)	74	79	74	Metals and ores and coffee
Costa Rica	98	93	82	Coffee, bananas, and cocoa
Cuba	91	94	86	Sugar, tobacco, and metallic ores
Ghana	91	85	84	Cocoa, diamonds, and manganese ore
Guatemala	88	91	69	Coffee, bananas, and cotton
Haiti	72	91	75	Coffee, sisal, and sugar
Honduras	87	76	66	Bananas and coffee
India	—	29	26	Tea, fibres, and cashew nuts
Indonesia	53	66	78	Rubber, petroleum, oil-seeds, and oils
Iran	—	41	57	Crude petroleum, cotton, and dried grapes
Iraq	81	96	98	Crude petroleum, dates, and barley
Ivory Coast	—	—	91	Coffee, cocoa, and wood
Jamaica	—	88	63	Metalliferous ores, sugar, and bananas
Kenya	51	52	68	Coffee, sisal, and tea
Malaya	71	62	64	Rubber and tin
Mexico	34	65	42	Cotton, non-ferrous metals and concentrates, and coffee
Morocco	36	45	49	Minerals, citrus fruits, and wheat
New Zealand	87	86	84	Wool, meat, and dairy products
Nigeria	87	74	69	Oil-seeds and oil, cocoa, and tin concentrates

(cont.) TABLE VI

*Percentage of total exports accounted for
by three principal commodities in:*

Country	1936–38	1953–55	1959–61	Commodities in 1959–61
Pakistan	—	86	58	Jute, cotton, and wool
Peru	80	64	63	Non-ferrous metals and ores, cotton, and sugar
Philippines	79	79	70	Coconut products, sugar, and timber
Rhodesia and Nyasaland	75	81	82	Copper, tobacco, and asbestos
South Africa	84	56	52	Gold, wool, and diamonds
Sudan	75	73	81	Cotton, gum arabic, and ground-nuts
Thailand	80	78	68	Rice, rubber, and tin ore
Tunisia	44	43	43	Phosphates, olive oil, and wheat
Turkey	42	58	52	Tobacco, cotton, and hazel nuts
Uganda	79	86	79	Cotton and coffee
UAR	78	87	78	Cotton and rice
Uruguay	70	80	81	Wool, meat, hides and skins
Venezuela	95	98	98	Petroleum, iron ore, and coffee

SOURCE: *U.N. World Economic Survey,* 1963
N.B. The percentages have not changed sharply since.

3) The reasons for this relative decline have already been described, but a summary here may be useful. It should include:

(*i*) The inheritance of North-South trading patterns from the colonial period during which the bulk of Atlantic investment overseas was devoted to the production of raw materials.

(*ii*) The persistence of tariff structures designed to perpetuate this pattern. Primary products usually enter developed markets tariff-free and the tariff rises with each level of working up—zero tariffs for raw materials, medium tariffs for semi-manufactures, higher tariffs for finished goods. The following example of two typical tariffs illustrates the trend in terms of the European Common Market's common external tariff which comes into force on July 1, 1968.

Product	Raw material (per cent)		Semi-manufactures (per cent)		Finished goods (per cent)	
Cocoa	beans	6.7	cocoa butter	20	powder	27 [a]
Hides	hides and				leather	
	skins	0	leather	10	goods	14–19 [a]

[a] These figures suggest too little protection. In many cases the tariff should really be estimated only on the "value added" where it is three times as high.

If these finished goods are still competitive—as with a wide range of textiles and garments—they are then excluded by quota. Thus the gains made in the process of manufacture tend to be chiefly harvested by the developed powers. In 1965 the less developed countries exported to the developed areas $21,800 million of primary products, but only $3,900 million of manufactures.

(iii) International trade has to be supported by a very wide range of services from which the earnings, termed "invisibles," can be very high. Shipping, banking, insurance, marketing—all these essential supporting services earned about $43,000 million for the developed nations in 1965 and virtually nothing for the developers, since 96 per cent of the world's shipping and just about 100 per cent of the world's insurance and international banking facilities are owned by firms in the developed nations.

(iv) These facts of history and policy are reinforced by some significant changes in the structure of developed economies. As their populations have stabilized and grown wealthier, developed nations' need for growing supplies of foodstuffs has slowed down. Moreover, they heavily protect their domestic farmers and tend to produce large grain surpluses. These surpluses are invaluable in times of famine and can, with care, be usefully integrated into local development and programs. But in some circumstances they may reduce the ability or the incentives in developing economies to modernize their own agriculture.

(v) Changes in technology, making for much fuller utilisation of raw materials and for the invention of a whole range of substitutes—plastics, petrochemicals, artificial rubber—can also depress the market for natural materials. And since all the world's funds for advanced research are concentrated in rich nations, it follows inevitably that a cheaper and more competitive use of the by-products of, say, a large chemical industry will be looked for and found more speedily than alternative ways of making up sisal or copra. Artificial rubber cuts back natural rubber, Atlantic-grown soya beans and their derivatives compete with Africa's groundnuts. Plastics and artificial fibres weaken cotton, wool, jute, cocoanut fibre. The balance of advantage in research expenditure is thus reflected in the higher competitiveness of products "invented" in developed lands.

(vi) There have been changes in the developing countries which also tend to increase the disequilibrium in world trade. With the coming of independence, many of them have plunged into increasing local production

of raw materials—cocoa, coffee, tea, bananas, sugar—
which are already grown mainly in developing lands.
The poor countries thus compete with each other. Supplies have increased sharply, far beyond the limits of
Western appetites. Coffee now has at least a year's supply
in storage and these carryovers depress prices further.

(*vii*) Poor countries are also handicapped in the expansion of manufactures for export since many such
goods demand mass production and hence a large market
if they are to be competitively produced. Local markets,
divided by scores of national sovereignties, are too
small for mass production. Car assembly plants in every
Latin American country, oil refineries in most African
states run at a loss. The dangers of industrialization in
these conditions include factories running below capacity and insufficient foreign exchange to buy spare parts
and materials. Such imbalances are accentuated further
when local governments, sometimes for purposes of
prestige, over-value their currencies or when they devote all their developmental energies to replacing imports, not seeking outlets for exports. Arms spending is
a general curse. Even a market as large as India's can
be held up by such obstacles in the early stages of
growth.

4) What can be done to lessen the imbalance of rewards in the world economy? The problem can be attacked from a number of angles:

a) *Tariffs and other forms of protection:*
The developed countries can do a number of things

to correct the bias in their tariff structures.

(*i*) They can admit a wide range of tropical products—cocoa, tea, coffee, tropical woods, bananas—tariff free. They can abolish all consumption taxes. The difficulty here is that some groups of countries—the African associates of the Common Market, some Commonwealth territories—enjoy preferences on these products and do not want to give away or share protected entry to Europe. Some Latin Americans therefore seek protected entry to the American market. A solution might lie, as is suggested in the Yaoundé Convention signed between the Common Market and its associates, in providing the countries which give up their preferences with direct financial support to assist local diversification. But Common Market countries are not yet willing to give up the protection they enjoy in Africa.

(*ii*) In the main, where general tariff reductions have been negotiated, the poorer nations might be permitted to keep their existing levels of protection for specified articles and for specified periods of time. Here the difficulties are the same as with any other weakening of the protection now enjoyed in wealthy countries.

(*iii*) The developing countries could be given general preferences for their manufactures and semi-manufactures. This would mean that the rich countries would levy lower tariffs on developing countries' goods than they do on each other.

(*iv*) In manufactures, the developed powers might go further and undertake a specific strategy designed to move themselves out of the simpler technologies—

in textiles, in semi-manufactures, in goods whose working up requires a lot of labour—and to buy these from the poorer lands. Once again, redeployment funds could be made available to Lyons or Lancashire or South Carolina as quotas and tariffs were removed. By shifting into more elaborate industries which do *not* require quota-protection, the areas would often find they had doubled profits and wage rates—this has been the post-textile experience of Massachusetts, for instance.

b) Guaranteed prices:

Commodity agreements which fix maximum prices and set up mechanisms for withholding stocks in years of high production and releasing them in low can give more stability to primary prices and have been tried, with varying degrees of success, in coffee, sugar, wheat, tin, tea and rubber. Attempts are now being made for a cocoa agreement. The difficulties are, first, to fix a range of prices high enough to reward producers and low enough not to discourage consumers; second, to persuade producers to stick to the export quotas which must be imposed if a commodity is in surplus; third, to devise and find the kind of diversification which will not renew the difficulties that arise, if, for example, all coffee producers diversify into tea, and tea growers in turn begin to face unsaleable surpluses; fourth, to finance the research into alternative uses either of the product itself or of the resources, capital, and labour used to produce it. Clearly, if the rich nations are prepared to finance diversification and research, agreements on price stabilization have a better chance of success.

One should also underline the fact that agreements made must, in the longer run, bear a reasonable relation to the state of world demand; assistance by the rich to increase consumption of tropical goods, for instance, by removing excise taxes, could usefully parallel the setting up of commodity agreements.

c) Compensatory finance:

(i) The International Monetary Fund at present runs a modest scheme whereby developing nations, facing a falling away in their earnings, can secure quickly and easily short term loans from the Fund to tide them over their difficulties. It is now suggested that such standby credits might be made available over, say, a ten-year period with easy terms of repayment.

(ii) A special fund under the direction of the World Bank on the order of $300–$400 million a year could be established to act as a further insurance against falls in export earnings over and above the levels that the IMF can finance. This proposal could also be supplemented by the so-called Horowitz Plan which proposes that the wealthy nations might subsidize the interest rates paid by poorer countries and reduce the pressures imposed by debt.

(iii) A much more ambitious scheme for permanent credit-creation has been discussed in the Stamp Plan and the Trifflin Plan. Its essence lies in increasing the working capital available for world trade (its "liquidity"). It suggests that fresh reserves be created each year to the value, say, of a 5 per cent increase in world trade and be made available in the first place to the developing nations. So far, the hostility of official banking circles in the developed world has overridden any such scheme on the grounds that it would be "inflationary." As a result of three years' discussion, a larger measure of liquidity is now to be introduced. But these new "drawing rights" on the IMF are related to the existing wealth of the participants and hence help the rich, not the poor nations. But there is no reason why this bias should not be corrected.

d) Common markets:

It has been shown since the Second World War that even nations as developed and sophisticated as those of Western Europe cannot take full advantage of the new technologies demanding massive research and investment and mass production unless their market transcends the old nationalist boundaries. The challenge is ever more acute to continents which include such ministates as Mauretania with 600,000 inhabitants or Laos with 2,070,000 or Costa Rica with 1,507,000. Common markets, with agreed strategies for development, are probably one of the preconditions of successful modernization as we move on towards the twenty-first century. Moreover, they can help to break the present dependence of developing nations on North-South trade and begin to expand trade with other developing peoples. Certainly where common markets are being tried, in

Western Europe, in Central America, or in East Africa, growth seems to be faster than in areas still fragmented by competitive sovereignties.